FEMINISTS SAY THE DARNDEST THINGS

FEMINISTS
Say the Darndest Things

A POLITICALLY INCORRECT PROFESSOR
CONFRONTS "WOMYN" ON CAMPUS

Mike Adams

Sentinel

SENTINEL
Published by the Penguin Group
Penguin Group (USA) Inc., 375 Hudson Street, New York, New York 10014, U.S.A. • Penguin Group (Canada), 90 Eglinton Avenue East, Suite 700, Toronto, Ontario, Canada M4P 2Y3 (a division of Pearson Penguin Canada Inc.) • Penguin Books Ltd, 80 Strand, London WC2R 0RL, England • Penguin Ireland, 25 St Stephen's Green, Dublin 2, Ireland (a division of Penguin Books Ltd) • Penguin Books Australia Ltd, 250 Camberwell Road, Camberwell, Victoria 3124, Australia (a division of Pearson Australia Group Pty Ltd) • Penguin Books India Pvt Ltd, 11 Community Centre, Panchsheel Park, New Delhi – 110 017, India • Penguin Group (NZ), 67 Apollo Drive, Rosedale, North Shore 0745, Auckland, New Zealand (a division of Pearson New Zealand Ltd) • Penguin Books (South Africa) (Pty) Ltd, 24 Sturdee Avenue, Rosebank, Johannesburg 2196, South Africa

Penguin Books Ltd, Registered Offices:
80 Strand, London WC2R 0RL, England

First published in 2007 by Sentinel,
a member of Penguin Group (USA) Inc.

1   3   5   7   9   10   8   6   4   2

LIBRARY OF CONGRESS CATALOGING-IN-PUBLICATION DATA
Adams, Mike S., 1964–
Feminists say the darndest things : a politically incorrect professor confronts "womyn" on campus / Mike S. Adams.
p.   cm.
ISBN 978-1-59523-042-3
1. Feminism. 2. Feminism and education. 3. Anti-feminism. I. Title.
HQ1155.A33 2007
306.43'2—dc22   2007005878

Printed in the United States of America
Set in Adobe Caslon
Designed by Daniel Lagin

To two old-school liberal Democrats: David L. McMillen,
the one who inspired me to become a college professor;
and Melvin C. Ray, the one who went out of his way to make sure that
my dreams of becoming a professor came true.

CONTENTS

PART II: WHY FEMINISTS HATE WOMEN WHO DON'T KILL CHILDREN   97

CONTENTS

NOTE TO THE READER

Due to the graphic language used by many feminists quoted in this book, the author and editorial staff have replaced such language with various icons, images, and abbreviations. We are sure, intelligent reader, that you will catch on quickly.

Also, it gives me unspeakable joy to sue many of these feminists mentioned in the book. I've decided that's the only language they understand. As should be clear in the text, some of the letters that follow were actually sent, and others were not. Some letters have been modified slightly for publication.

ACKNOWLEDGMENTS

FIRST, I MUST THANK DAVID FRENCH FOR A PHONE CALL HE made to me in December 2005. That call led to a decision to coauthor a book, which, in turn, led me to my agent, D.J. Snell. D.J. suggested that—in addition to the book David and I were writing—we each submit a solo-authored manuscript. Thanks to Bernadette Serton and the nice folks at Penguin you are now reading my published "solo" manuscript.

I would like to thank the kind folks at Springfield Armory for making great guns and for giving me free ones. A similar tip of the hat goes to the folks at La Flor Dominicana. I love their cigars, especially when they're free. I'll be expecting a free box for every thousand copies this book ends up selling.

Also, I give a big thanks to the people at Salem Communications, who pay me to write columns. Without them I wouldn't have so many readers sending me free guns and free cigars.

I would also like to thank Wal-Mart for its persistent exploitation of cheap Asian labor. That exploitation really helps bring down the price of ammunition.

Thanks to Pat Coyle at the Young America's Foundation. Without him, every one of my speeches about free speech would be a free speech. Now that I'm getting paid for these speeches, I can hire illegal aliens to do all the things I don't want to do around the house.

And thanks to all of those people who are responsible for global warming. I really like global warming because I hate the cold and I'm really not concerned about future generations. I hope this isn't offensive or hurtful to those of you who have grandchildren.

Finally, thanks to Phyllis Schlafly for her kind words of encouragement. Because of her support, I have come to realize that criticizing feminism is one of my greatest gifts. Maybe that's because it's so easy to do. Regardless, it sure is a fun way to make a living.

FEMINISTS SAY THE DARNDEST THINGS

INTRODUCTION

***

Some time around 3:00 p.m., february 20, 2006:
As I write the opening lines of my second book, I am sitting in my office at the University of North Carolina-Wilmington with a nagging headache. It probably wasn't caused by the giant poster of a condom hanging on my office door. I think the poster—placed there by a campus feminist group—is kind of funny. Under the condom it says: "If she's feeling spunky, better wrap up your monkey." You have to admit it. That's kind of funny.

Nor do I think the cause of my headache is the bickering I just heard during a lecture by a job candidate—one who just happens to be a feminist. During the question-and-answer session following her lecture, two women got into an argument. One said that women are just as likely to engage in domestic violence as men. That made the other woman, a feminist professor, violently angry. She insisted that domestic violence is "male dominated." She thinks that everything bad is "male dominated." But that's not the cause of my headache. Headaches are bad so it must be a man's fault.

I don't even think my headache is related to the emergency faculty meeting just scheduled via e-mail by our chair, who just happens to be a feminist. The meeting is being called to discuss a division in our department caused by two Marxist professors who are supposedly trying to turn our proposed graduate program into a "Critical Criminology" program. For those of you who don't know, "critical" is a code word for "communist." I wasn't going to mention it, but the two Marxists just happen to be feminists.

Maybe the source of my headache is the recent letter, written by a feminist to my dean and my chancellor, who also happens to be a feminist, calling for me to be fired. She wrote the letter because I wrote a little paragraph in my nationally published column suggesting feminists are intolerant of free speech. Maybe I shouldn't be allowed to say that.

Come to think of it, there is so much lunacy on this campus that is caused by feminists that there's really no way I'll ever pinpoint the exact cause of my headache. So I'll just put aside my concerns with this nagging headache and get down to the reason I'm writing this book about feminists. It's one that can be summarized in a single sentence:

I want to find out why they hate us.

Indeed, feminists are among the most hateful creatures on this planet. Since they haven't flown any planes into skyscrapers (at least not yet), we can't actually declare war on them. So maybe we should just borrow a line from campus liberals and simply find out why "they" hate "us."

Before I really get going, I want to make it clear that by "us" I don't just mean men. Feminists hate women, too. That is, they hate all women who aren't feminists. And these pro-choicers seem undeterred by the fact that three out of every four women choose not to identify with the term "feminist."

When you consider the proportion of women these feminists hate (around 75 percent) and the proportion of men they hate (around 100 percent), it soon becomes apparent that feminists only get along with about 12.5 percent of the population—that is, other feminists united in their hatred of the majority. In other words, I probably have my work cut out for me.

Since my task is so daunting, I've decided to seek plenty of outside input by conducting extensive interviews with feminists on a wide range of topics. That way, I can listen to their feelings (often in the form of rage) on a wide range of topics as the feminists themselves help answer important questions like:

- Why do feminists hate men (especially the ones with a sense of humor)?
- Why do feminists hate unborn children (especially their own)?
- Why do feminists hate gun owners (with the possible exception of Muslim fundamentalists)?
- Why do feminists hate capitalists?
- Why do feminists hate Christian fundamentalists (instead of Muslim fundamentalists)?
- Why do feminists hate Republicans?
- Why do feminists hate traditional women (especially the pretty ones)?

Although this book's "why do they hate us" theme is borrowed from liberals, the methodology is not. Unlike most liberals, I intend to reveal all of my biases on this controversial subject beforehand. Then I will demonstrate—only after giving the feminists a chance to explain themselves—that I was right to draw certain conclusions about feminism and feminists over the course of my career as a conservative professor. The following is a list of those conclusions, which reveal all of my personal biases on the topic of feminism:

1. *Modern feminism is not a political ideology or philosophy.*

American feminists generally do not become feminists because of some well-defined political goal. Feminists want to vote. They want to be free to hold elective office. They want rape to be illegal. They want to be able to work. They don't want to be forced to get and stay pregnant at all times. They want genital mutilation (of females) to be illegal.

I have an important newsflash for these feminists: They have already achieved all of these political objectives. But, nonetheless, they continue to "demand" these rights—almost as steadfastly as they "demand" to be taken seriously. Therefore, most feminists continue to live in the past without being taken seriously in the present.

2. *Most feminists don't really want equality.*

Recently, one of the stars of *The Vagina Monologues* wrote me complaining about a column I published criticizing that infamous feminist play. She told me she was "offended" and "hurt" by my critique. Naturally, I asked her whether the flashing "vagina" sign advertising the play in front of our school was offensive. I reminded her that the Greek Orthodox and Baptist churches were located right across from the sign. She responded by saying that she "didn't give a s#*t" what they thought.

Another example comes from a former secretary in my department. One day she left work crying because I criticized campus feminists (for hanging racist posters on campus showing Condi Rice standing in a cage holding a bunch of bananas). The next week she was back in the office tearlessly criticizing her husband for his poor sexual performance.

Increasingly, these campus feminists strive to be (a) constantly offended, and (b) constantly offensive. One unanticipated consequence of the feminists' unequal application of the "right to be unoffended" is that many people now deem feminists to be emotionally inferior to the rest of us.

3. *The feminist love of postmodernism has resulted in widespread academic and personal dishonesty.*

A few years ago, I began to realize that one can seldom trust a feminist to tell the truth. For example, I once asked a feminist to debate me on the issue of abortion. She told me she really wasn't pro-choice. I did an Internet search and found that she had repeatedly referred to herself as "pro-choice" on feminist list serves. She made those references to herself both before and after our conversation. In other words, she lied.

When I asked another feminist to debate me on abortion she said that she didn't discuss such personal topics publicly. But then I read her autobiography. After talking about losing her virginity—including details about how she cleaned the blood off the couch afterwards—she dedicated countless pages to the issue of abortion and how a "lack of choice" adversely affects young women.

After reading on, I realized why she didn't tell the truth. She revealed that she was a postmodernist who didn't even like to use the word "truth."

When I later found myself in an argument with a feminist—about whether a female student who lied about a rape to get out of taking a test should be expelled—I understood the postmodern feminist position better. Feminists just can't help but lie because there is no such thing as the truth. That's what they tell us but no one really knows whether it's true.

4. *Most feminists do not have a sense of humor.*

You've probably heard the one about the guy who asked a feminist "How many feminists does it take to screw in a lightbulb." Her answer was "That's not funny!"

I thought about that joke after an antifeminist student (a woman) put a bumper sticker on my door saying "So you're a feminist ... isn't that cute."

When a feminist student was offended, she decided that the whole administration, including the board of trustees, needed to know about it. She was furious. So she had her dad write the letter for her. *I am woman hear me roar, and my daddy fights my wars!*

And speaking of war, there was also the time I dressed as an Iraqi woman in order to sneak into an antiwar protest. I was dressed to kill, including a burka and sandals. I also had a sign saying "I want to be raped, gassed, and tortured by Saddam's thugs! So, please, don't help me, America!"

Everyone who saw me in that outfit thought it was hilarious. The only ones who were angry were a handful of feminist faculty members.

5. *Feminists are less concerned with women's rights than they are with their own right to have an abortion.*

George W. Bush has done more for women's rights than any president in modern history. But feminists hate him because he is opposed to abortion rights.

Bill Clinton sexually harassed more women than any president in American history. But that's okay. He supports abortion rights so feminists love him. If he were ever convicted of rape, feminists would still love him because he supports abortion rights.

6. *Feminists really don't care about racism.*

Feminists often quote statistics about the underrepresentation of women in certain occupations as if this is "conclusive proof" of sexism. They don't need to rely on specific evidence in individual cases. However, when confronted with statistics showing that the majority of abortions are performed on blacks and Hispanics, they remain mute. Surely they know that most people in this country are white. And Planned Parenthood will play a larger role in keeping it that way than the Ku Klux Klan ever dreamed of playing.

Genocide is a terrible thing to most feminists. But the loss of "reproductive choice" is even worse.

7. *Feminists generally lack the courage to act as individuals.*

My first college free speech controversy involved a business professor who tried to stop the student newspaper from publishing a column called the "sexual horoscopes." He claimed that the column was "indecent." Then he tried to set up a panel to filter "indecent" material before the student paper went to press. I took him on in front of the Faculty Senate and won.

But before I won there was a vigorous debate on the Faculty Senate e-mail list. It went on for days before someone made the observation that all of the participants in the debate were males. A few days later, a feminist group published a joint response signed by about two dozen feminists.

I saw the significance of this pattern immediately. The men all had individual opinions. The feminists all had the same opinion. The men embraced individualism. The feminists embraced collectivism. They can't seem to do or say anything without the emotional support of their sisters.

8. *When faced with uncertainty, feminists have less self-control than hunters.*

Once, when I was deer-hunting in Ivanhoe, North Carolina, I saw something moving in the brush about 100 yards away. It was foggy outside and I was looking through a 4 X 32 scope mounted on a Marlin 30-30. I never take a shot over 100 yards with that little brush gun. And I never shoot at anything unless I know exactly what is out there.

That day I got to thinking about the feminist approach to abortion. Feminists often justify abortion by saying that the procedure is no different from picking a scab. That's when I start asking questions.

I often ask feminists about a film I saw of a fetus in the first trimester of development. The baby was yawning, rubbing its eyes, and even rolling around and playing in the womb. I like to ask feminists whether they have ever seen a scab yawn.

When I press them on the issue, they seldom admit that the fetus is a person. But they seldom state unequivocally that it is not. They usually say they "don't know for sure." And they say that I don't know for sure, either.

That really epitomizes our differences. When I know it is a deer in the brush, I pull the trigger. When I know it is a human, I hold my fire. When I don't know, I also hold my fire.

The feminist who "doesn't know" whether it is a person has the abortion anyway. She just pulls the trigger. That really says it all, doesn't it?

9. *Feminists cannot grasp the importance of gradual self-disclosure.*

Long before I earned a master's degree in social psychology, I learned that one of the keys to successful relationships is choosing the appropriate pace of self-disclosure. If you too rapidly reveal intimate details of your personal life, people tend to devalue your friendship. If you reveal things more slowly, stronger relationships tend to follow.

People are often turned off to feminism because feminists tend to reveal intimate details of their lives very quickly. This is especially true of feminist professors in the classroom. The following complaint from a college student is illustrative:

> Dr. Adams: I agree with your observations on feminism. I took an English class taught by a feminist who I liked very much at first. When she started complaining about her first husband I felt sorry for her. By the time she started attacking her fifth husband I wanted to withdraw from the course. I have no idea how many different times she's been married. I just know that none of the divorces were her fault. She didn't seem to understand that there was one common element in all of her dysfunctional relationships. The common element was her.

Sadly, it gets much worse than that in the feminist classroom. Feminist professors also discuss their sexual experiences—consensual and nonconsensual—in excruciating detail in public. Venues include the classroom, books, and sometimes "scholarly" journals. The First Amendment gives them the right to reveal what most people would say is "too much information." But it does not give them the right to be taken seriously in the aftermath.

10. *Feminist-sponsored masturbation workshops on college campuses.*

If a feminist needs a workshop to learn how to masturbate, it is safe to conclude that she is really uptight.

II. *Feminists would rather solve a problem by changing "society" than by changing their own behavior.*

One obvious example of this is "love your body" day—not to be confused with "masturbation workshop" day. At many universities, "love your body" day concludes with the feminists holding a beauty pageant featuring overweight models—usually with pretty faces. The purpose of this is to convince us that bigger women are just as attractive as smaller (by this, they mean thinner) women.

Sociology professors often pursue the notion that beauty is not objective but "socially constructed" by showing their students medieval paintings of nude, pudgy women. The argument is that fat used to be considered attractive. Therefore, it can be that way in the future with enough social engineering. So, feminists seek nothing less than to change societal perceptions of beauty with millions of dollars of taxpayer-funded programs.

But I have a question: Wouldn't it just be easier to exercise?

Along the same lines, have you noticed how chic it has become for feminists to claim they are Marxists? Feminist professors spend a good bit of time trying to persuade their students that Marxism is the answer to America's problems.

If a woman's opportunities are better under communism, wouldn't it be easier to get a job at the University of Havana than to start a bloody Marxist revolution?

I've never seen a bunch of poor, oppressed feminists board a leaky boat in Miami in order to paddle their way to freedom in Castro's Cuba. But I do have a few friends in south Florida who escaped from communism. They still have their boats. We would be proud to give these Marxist feminists a lift to Havana any time.

12. *The four most common words a feminist uses are "I," "me," "my," and "mine."*

I really get tired of hearing these four words from feminists. "I feel this" or "I feel that." "Keep your laws off *my* body." "It's *my* body, *my* choice." Feminists are the only people in society who actually use these four words more in adulthood than they did when they were two-year-olds.

It is especially irritating when they say that the man should have no right to be involved in the decision to abort. They remind us that a man's opinion is irrelevant by simply repeating the phrase "It's *my* body." But should that logic apply when the aborted baby is a male? What happens after the abortion is performed and one looks into the bucket and sees a little penis? Whose penis is it? Is it the woman's penis?

13. *Feminist positions on abortion and capital punishment cannot be reconciled.*

As I mention before, feminists often support the decision to abort a fetus even though they admit that they "don't know" whether "it" is a person. They will admit that "it" eventually becomes a person with rights. But now that partial birth abortion is becoming more defensible in the minds of feminists, it's hard to tell when they think personhood begins. I can hardly pin a feminist down on this issue. All I know is that "it" can count on feminist support with absolute certainty only after "it" commits a murder.

14. *Feminists' husbands are even more irritating than feminists.*

I mentioned earlier a free speech debate on my campus. A bunch of men debated a point for several days. When they were done, a campus feminist coalition issued a joint statement of their "collective" opinion.

But there is one part of the story I omitted. After the feminists issued their statement, the husband of the head feminist issued his individual opinion on the matter, which happened to reflect complete agreement with his wife. This "man" was afraid to express his opinion until after he knew what his feminist wife thought—or, more accurately, felt.

Or maybe I'm wrong. Perhaps he just thought that a little more kissing would make him different from all the other men his feminist wife had previously divorced (there were four).

But that man is not the biggest pansy I've ever seen. That award goes to a guy whose feminist wife was rumored to be sleeping with one of my colleagues. After he got a few drinks under his belt one night, he told me that he wouldn't mind if his wife was having an affair. He said their friendship was strong enough to endure it. Well, how liberating! He's going to support her through thick and thin—even if another man is hiding his hoo-hoo dilly in her cha-cha.

15. *Feminists can't face the reality of "gender-ocide."*

It's bad enough that feminists are silent on the issue of minority over representation in abortion clinics. But their heartlessness is compounded by the fact that they seldom discuss statistics indicating that every year more girls are aborted worldwide than boys. There is no question that this is the case. The only question is exactly how many more millions of girls are aborted per year.

And so they leave it to the antifeminists to ask the hard questions, to combat sexism, and to combat what some now call "gender-ocide."

16. *It doesn't take much intellectual firepower to become a feminist scholar.*

I once told a feminist that the term "feminist scholar" was an oxymoron. She asked me what I meant by the term "oxymoron." That's almost as bad as those masturbation workshops I mentioned earlier.

If you need to hold a workshop to learn how to masturbate, you aren't terribly bright. Remember, feminists are trying to make the case that a woman can do anything as well as a man. That's the main thesis of feminism. Yet, somehow, men are fully capable of masturbating without taking a seminar. For men, it's a natural talent. For campus feminists, it's another excuse to seek funding from the university administration.

17. *Feminists have an affinity for communism.*

I used to get really angry with feminists over their alliance with communism. After all, I've had relatives who risked their lives to fight in wars rolling back the forces of communism and fascism. Many of you know people who gave their very lives to defeat such forces. When you see these historically ignorant feminists embrace the very ideas that once threatened our precious freedoms, you probably get mad, too.

But now I kind of like the idea that these feminists are waving flags that feature a hammer and sickle. It really makes sense to me. After all, the communists killed 100 million innocents in just seventy-two years. One-third of a century after *Roe v. Wade*, the feminists are on a pace to kill even more innocents. To be precise, the projected total of abortions in America by 2045 (that's seventy-two years after *Roe*) is 102,545,450.

Maybe, after they break the communist murder record, feminists can come up with their own flag. Instead of a hammer and sickle, it can feature a scalpel and a suction tube.

18. *Feminists are trying to destroy the American family.*

A few years ago, Peter Kreeft wrote a great book called *How to Win the Culture War*. In the book he argued that attacking marriage was essential for those who wished to radically transform (read: destroy) the foundations of our society. You can't just tear down a whole society. You have to weaken individual communities. But that involves weakening families. And that, in turn, involves weakening marriages. According to Kreeft, the best way to weaken marriages is to encourage adultery. This is easy to do when people begin to worship sex.

So when parents drop their kids off for orientation at a school like Rice University, there is always some feminist there to encourage them to "explore their sexual freedom." That means have sex with anyone and everyone. And when they take Sociology 101, the feminist professor is there to tell them that marriage is a good deal for men but not for women.

19. *Feminists are the biggest censors on college campuses today.*

Maybe it was the time that a feminist tried to kick one of my former students out of her women's studies class for laughing at one of her ideas. The professor didn't even hear him. Another feminist, a student in the class, did and reported him to the professor.

Or maybe it was the time I ridiculed a feminist Marxist's essay on 9/11 and the author's mother spent three weeks trying to have me disciplined by the administration.

Or maybe it was the time I made fun of an antiwar feminist. I said that if she would shave her armpits, people would be more likely to read her antiwar sign when she held it up. As it stood, people were just staring at her hairy armpits. I was just trying to be helpful. But unfortunately her feminist friend sent someone into a board of trustees meeting with a plea to have me disciplined for making fun of her friend's armpits. Fortunately, the plea was ignored.

To tell you the truth, I don't know when it was. But I have definitely realized that feminists are the biggest censors on my campus. And they are always driven to censor those who do not take them seriously—just to punish them for the crime of not taking them seriously.

20. *Feminists frequently confuse positive and inverse correlations.*

Here are two frequent examples:

> The number of abortions a woman has positively correlates with her personal happiness.
> The number of sex partners a woman has positively correlates with her self-esteem.

Sexual freedom and reproductive choice are, in fact, related to happiness and self-esteem. But the feminists have the relationships backward. That's why the key to raising a happy daughter is to focus on two things: have her watch everything the feminists do; and tell her to do the exact opposite.

That pretty well sums up my biases on the topic at hand. Now that I've laid those biases out on the table, it's time to demonstrate that they are accurate by listening closely to what feminists have to say on a variety of topics. This shouldn't be hard to do. In fact, just logging on to one of the Women's Resource Center (WRC) websites here in the UNC system provides enough information to confirm many of my conclusions. For example, here are some quotes from the Appalachian State University WRC website:

> "A woman without a man is like a fish without a bicycle."
>
> —GLORIA STEINEM

> "Whatever women do they must do twice as well as men to be thought half as good. Luckily, this is not difficult."
>
> —CHARLOTTE WHITTON

> "Sure, God created man before woman. But then you always make a rough draft before the final masterpiece."
>
> —ANONYMOUS

> "If women are supposed to be less rational and more emotional at the beginning of our menstrual cycle when the female hormone is at its lowest level, then why isn't it logical to say that, in those few days, women behave the most like the way men behave all month long?"
>
> —GLORIA STEINEM

> "Can you imagine a world without men? No crime and lots of happy fat women."
>
> —NICOLE HOLLANDER

> "A man's got to do what a man's got to do. A woman must do what he can't."
>
> —RHONDA HANSOMS

> "Behind every successful man is a surprised woman."
>
> -MARYON PEARSON

The first part of this book will explore an issue reflected in many of those quotes—the feminist hatred of men. The first chapter is a letter to a Marxist feminist colleague of mine here at UNC-Wilmington. It was inspired by a conversation I recently overheard between her and a nonfeminist as they were talking in the women's restroom—the one that is right next to my office with the very thin walls.

Of course, the Marxist feminist doesn't know the walls are that thin, otherwise she wouldn't have said everything she said about me in the restroom. Of course, I hope she doesn't mind that I was eavesdropping on her. She said something so interesting that I simply can't stall my inquiry any longer. I simply have to write.

Hopefully, she and all the other feminists in these pages will take the time to respond. If not, at least I can say I gave them a chance. They certainly have a "right to choose" one way or the other. Either way, this promises to be a lot of fun.

PART I

Why Feminists Hate Men Who Aren't Gay

I

GOSH, IDIOT!

Hello Donna.

I wanted to write you this short letter while some of the comments you made a few days ago are still fresh in my mind. You will recall that you recently overheard a short conversation I had with one of the department secretaries. She saw me walking away from the men's restroom while she was walking toward the women's restroom. You were headed there, too.

Don't worry, Donna, I'm not going to argue whether the lack of a third bathroom—one for those who are "questioning" their gender— is an example of "heterosexist" oppression, a view held by a number of transgender rights advocates. We can flush that issue out later. Right now I want to ask you why you considered my remarks to the secretary to be a form of harassment, perhaps the kind that should be dealt with formally by the university.

You will recall that the "harassing" remark in question came shortly after the secretary teased me for carrying my toothbrush and toothpaste out of the men's restroom. After she made her joking remark—something about the tooth fairy that I'm surprised you didn't deem "homophobic" harassment—I responded by calling her an "idiot." Actually, the two words "gosh" and "idiot" were all I said to her.

Donna, there are exactly three reasons why you should have known that this was a form of humor rather than a form of workplace harassment, although I recognize that your status as a feminist makes it difficult for you to discern humor, no matter how obvious:

First, you are a self-proclaimed scholar in the sociology of "popular culture." Anyone who claims to be an expert in popular culture should be familiar with very popular movies. One of the most popular movies among college students today is called *Napoleon Dynamite*, the name of its protagonist. One of the phrases he repeats, usually under his breath in a self-deprecating manner, is "Gosh, idiot." That's why you see kids walking around campus wearing T-shirts that say "Gosh, idiot." When I uttered the phrase "Gosh, idiot," I was making fun of a male actor, not a female secretary.

Come to think of it, you could say that the phrase "Gosh, idiot" has been repeated so often that it has become a part of our popular culture. Of course, to say that, you would have to have some familiarity with popular culture. Everyone in the vicinity of the bathrooms understood the pop culture reference except for the feminist with the Ph.D. who is a self-proclaimed expert in popular culture. I'll resist the temptation to repeat the phrase until I've cleared myself of the potential charge of workplace harassment.

The second reason you should have seen this situation as one involving humor, as opposed to harassment, is the day-to-day relationship I have with the secretary in question. We've been good friends for years as evidenced by the fact that we shoot the breeze in the office on a daily basis.

In the midst of those daily bull sessions, I am often asked by the "harassed" secretary to perform one of my numerous political or celebrity impersonations. Since you've worked with me for over a decade, you are undoubtedly aware that I do dozens of these impersonations.

People around the office often ask me to do impressions of political figures like George H.W. Bush, Al Gore Jr., or Ross Perot. I also do impressions of celebrities like Truman Capote—and, of course, the one I was doing in the hall that caused our little misunderstanding.

This is all information that could have helped you to more accurately assess the situation you mistakenly dubbed as a form of harassment. But the real problem is that the information is inaccessible to you because, in my opinion, you don't spend enough time at work. I have a theory about why Marxist feminists rarely spend even twenty hours a week at the office, but I'll have to explain that later.

The third reason you should have seen this as a humorous, but not harassing, situation is that the secretary literally doubled over in laughter as soon as I made the remark that offended you. When she actually stopped and placed both hands on her knees and laughed until her face turned red, you should have known that everything was okay.

But you didn't.

Instead, you followed her into the bathroom and started to talk to her about the concept of workplace harassment. That was right before you told her she "didn't have to take that" kind of treatment from Mike Adams. I know this because my office is right next to the women's restroom and I can hear everything you say in there. In fact, I've been listening to your potty talk for years.

So, in addition to your lack of understanding of popular culture, your lack of understanding of my relationship with the "victim," and your lack of understanding of the concept of nonverbal communication, we must add the following item to your list of shortcomings: You lack understanding of the extent to which sound travels through the thin walls that line the halls of the Department of Sociology and Criminal Justice at UNC-Wilmington.

As bad as all this sounds, Donna, I have an even bigger problem with your silly ploy to have me accused of harassment. It has to do with rape. But I'll let you digest this first letter before I write back tomorrow.

Update: Several letters in this book were addressed to Donna. She responded to the first letter Dr. Adams sent to her, which appears later in the book. However, after the first was sent, Dr. Adams decided to file a federal lawsuit against three feminists in this book. Because Donna will be a likely witness at the trial, none of the other letters were sent. Nonetheless, they are reprinted, (a) for your pure enjoyment, and (b) for their educational value as tools to expose feminist intolerance.

2

WHEN FEMINISTS CRY "RAPE"

Hello again, Donna:

I hope you've had an opportunity to digest some of what I wrote to you yesterday. Some of my words may have sounded harsh. But they aren't as harsh as what I have to say to you today.

The silliness of your recent conduct in the women's restroom cannot be fully appreciated without revisiting a conversation we had several years ago. I'm sure you remember the disagreement we had about the student who concocted a false rape story just to get out of taking one of my exams. When she said she had to go to the hospital to visit her sister in Winston-Salem, North Carolina—whom she claimed was nearly beaten to death by a rapist—I knew she was lying to me. In fact, I had caught this student lying to me before.

Nonetheless, when I called her on the lie, she publicly defamed me by rushing into the Dean of Student's Office accusing me of some form of patriarchal oppression—all for refusing to believe her obvious lie. She castigated me so badly that the director of Greek affairs called my office to criticize me for refusing to allow the student to make up the exam at a later date.

For a while there I was looking like an insensitive jerk. That was before a nonfeminist employee in the Dean's Office intervened. Suspecting that the student was lying, she asked a few pointed questions and the girl's story fell apart completely.

Of course, rather than apologize for causing such a complete disruption at the end of the semester—and for besmirching my reputation—the student gave me a sarcastic Hallmark card. The card she taped to my office door said "I'm Sorry" on the outside. On the inside, the student wrote "I'm sorry that you thought I was lying, Dr. Adams."

It's really hard to top that kind of feminist audacity. But somehow you managed to do it, Donna, when you actually defended the girl. You will recall that you actually took the position that she should not have been disciplined in any way by the university as a result of her actions. But, unfortunately, that wasn't quite the peak of your audacity.

Later we discussed another case involving a student who claimed that she (not her sister) was raped on campus. She actually wasted police resources by launching a phony investigation just to get out of an exam. That was when your insolence reached a new level.

With a straight face, you actually looked at me and said that she, too, should get off without punishment. This was despite the fact that she actually identified another student by name and accused him of rape.

Just after we finished our conversation, the only Republican woman in the department—this was before she was denied tenure, in part, for not being a feminist—called me into her office. Her only comment was "Your penis is too big for Donna."

The comment sounds crude and strange at first. But her point, which was actually twofold, can be summarized as: Donna hates men in general, and Donna hates men like you—gun-toting, capitalist, Christian, Republicans—even more.

I made a serious mistake, Donna, by actually defending you on both counts. I mistakenly suggested that you were just trying to be lenient toward the students because you have a soft spot and think that young people who make mistakes should be given a second chance.

But now, after your comments in the bathroom, I've had a change of heart. Clearly, no matter what the subject, you always side with the woman and against the man. Certainly, no one in her right mind could argue that calling someone a "rapist" should go unpunished while calling someone an "idiot" should be punished as harassment.

Donna, you know as well as I do that only someone in her left mind could make such an argument. Only a far-left, man-hating feminist could be so lost, so arrogant, and so full of irrational bigotry.

Update: Donna teaches a course on media and popular culture. One major contention—often repeated in her lectures—is that the Fox News Channel is "biased."

3

I FOUND MY THRILL
IN FRONT OF ANITA HILL

Hᴇʟʟᴏ ᴄʜᴀɴᴄᴇʟʟᴏʀ ᴅᴇᴘᴀᴏʟᴏ:

I was looking on the university website the other day when I came across your vita on the chancellor's page. I noticed you have all your academic accomplishments listed for each of the institutions at which you were previously employed. More than anything else, I noticed that you initiated the Sexual Harassment Task Force at Augusta College in the 1980s. I also noticed you served on the task force from 1987 to 1990.

This is really quite an accomplishment, since it predates the Anita Hill/Clarence Thomas controversy. No one can say you were jumping on the bandwagon with the harassment issue since you initiated this task force four years before the Thomas hearings. Your foresight probably helped you get a job as president of our university. And this definitely makes you an expert on sexual harassment. I hope you don't mind if I ask you a few questions on the topic, given your obvious expertise.

First, I'd like to ask you about our new harassment policy, which I have reproduced below for your convenience:

> *Harassment is unwelcome conduct based on race, color, religion, creed, sex, national origin, age, disability, veteran status or sexual orientation that is either a condition of working or learning ("quid pro quo") or creates a hostile environment.*

The reason I'm asking about the new policy is that I recently received a very disturbing e-mail from a feminist student. In the e-mail the student talked about her vagina using fairly graphic terminology. She also talked about her propensity to discuss her vagina with other feminist students. I think a little background information is in order.

It seems the student who wrote me that disturbing e-mail was one of the stars of the play *The Vagina Monologues*. This play, which, among other things, encourages women to sit around and talk about their genitalia, was not taken very seriously a few years ago. But when you decided to attend the play—and to allow yourself to be introduced to the audience by a group of feminists called the Vagina Warriors—you may have caused others to take it more seriously.

Because of your leadership, Chancellor DePaolo, more and more young women are sitting around talking about their vaginas. But the crucial question is whether they can talk about their vaginas to people who don't want to hear about them, particularly people who can't understand all the fuss because they don't have vaginas of their own.

This is where the harassment code comes into play. Specifically, I am asking you to send a memo to all faculty, staff, and students urging them to refrain from sending people unwelcome e-mails describing their genitals. I would like you to specifically threaten them with formal disciplinary action under the new harassment code if they disobey your warning.

I know this request is unusual but, please, ask yourself the following questions as you consider my request:

1. What could be more unwelcome than getting an e-mail from a feminist talking about her vagina?
2. Morally speaking, is it any better than getting an e-mail from an antifeminist calling his penis "long dong silver"?
3. And, finally, have you forgotten what the Clarence Thomas controversy was all about?

Thank you for your kind consideration.

Update: Dr. Adams never heard back from Rosemary DePaolo. Instead, she had the director of human resources contact him to discuss his concerns. Undeterred, Adams would try to get a response out of Chancellor DePaolo again. Stay tuned as the drama unfolds.

4

MUCH ADO
ABOUT SOMETHING

―――――――

Dear falsely accused professor:

I want to start my response to your letter by assuring you that, despite your carelessness, you're not going to be adversely affected by the recent accusation of "hostile environment" harassment that has been maliciously levied against you. Before I give you the good news, let me explain what you did wrong and how it helped precipitate this unfortunate situation.

Of course, there is absolutely nothing wrong with your decision to date a girl who is only twenty-three years old—even though she graduated from your university only a few months ago. After all, you are only thirty-one years old and, according to your account, you didn't meet the girl until several weeks after her graduation from the university. Obviously, your relationship presents no conflict of interest with your duties as a professor.

Nor is there anything wrong with her decision to visit you at work the other day. But it was probably a bad idea—a very bad idea—for your girlfriend to kiss you in the hallway between classes while she was wearing a sweatshirt that had the letters of her old sorority sewn on the front.

―――――――

In your letter, I noticed that you described your girlfriend as being just over five feet tall and weighting about ninety-five pounds. So, I am left wondering whether you were just asking for a campus-wide rumor to be spread about you. In other words, did you not even consider the possibility that some onlookers would reasonably conclude that you were involved with a sorority girl who is still an undergraduate?

But, despite your carelessness, the even greater carelessness of your feminist accuser is going to get you off the hook—at least this time. That carelessness was first exhibited when she called the Dean's Office to report you for accepting a kiss from a girl wearing an "Alpha Phi" sweatshirt. And this is where you also got a little lucky.

Fortunately, the dean who heard these accusations is not a feminist. He is a man with a Ph.D. in one of the real sciences—as opposed to the "social sciences" or humanities. Therefore, he was bright enough to ask a few pointed questions when your accuser was unable to produce your girlfriend's name. In addition to telling the feminist not to call back until she had specific information, he gave your male department chair a call, which allowed him to give you a "head's up" warning as the situation developed.

Of course, we both know how feminists act when they are chastised, even mildly chastised, for doing something dumb. They lose control of their emotions and end up doing something even dumber. Your accuser provides us with no exception to the rule.

When the dean got a second call accusing you of creating a "hostile environment," your accuser actually offered the name of a young woman who was allegedly seen drinking with you in a bar about a year ago. A brief investigation revealed that your drinking partner was of legal drinking age and, once again, she was a college graduate.

Shortly thereafter, your feminist accuser was politely told to "get lost" a second time. The bad news is that she is now twice as dangerous since she has been embarrassed twice by your dean. I wouldn't be surprised if she accused him of creating a "hostile environment" for actually daring to ask questions about her baseless accusations.

You are simply incredibly lucky that I happen to know this woman who falsely accused you. With your permission, I'd like to write her personally to ask a few questions about sexual harassment in general and your case in particular.

Update: The falsely accused professor gave his consent for the following letter.

5

THE HO' TELL MOTEL

Good morning, my esteemed feminist colleague.

I had an interesting conversation the other night while I was sitting in a bar with an undercover vice and narcotics agent. I've been helping him lately raid crack houses where suspects are using and dealing drugs in violation of their parole agreements. The work can be stressful so sometimes we go out and grab a beer afterward.

The other night after a few drinks the officer started laughing about an embarrassing scene that took place when a male candidate interviewed for a job at UNC-Wilmington. It seems the officer had heard—directly from you, no less—that you and another feminist wound up at the hotel room of the job candidate at the same time. The officer furthermore quotes you as saying "She (the other feminist, that is) tried to steal my boyfriend."

This is a big problem for you because this is now the second credible source quoting you as admitting to an amorous relationship with a job candidate. In my view there are two possible ways to interpret the situation:

---

1. *You are actually telling the truth about your romantic and/or sexual liaison with the job candidate.* If so, this means you are guilty of quid pro quo sexual harassment. Certainly no man in such a situation could voluntarily submit to your sexual advances. He could hardly say "no" for fear that you would vote against him when the committee fills the position for which he interviewed.

2. *You are lying about your romantic and/or sexual liaison with the job candidate.* If you are lying about this liaison, you have created a "hostile environment" by sharing your false stories with faculty and students. Surely, reasonable men hearing such stories would feel uncomfortable in an environment in which they merely perceived a requirement to sleep with feminists in order to get ahead.

I'm going to surprise you today by coming to your defense. I think you are lying about this hotel incident. That means you aren't guilty of quid pro quo sexual harassment. This is important because the alternative—a charge of "hostile environment" harassment—is far more difficult to prove.

But before I go today, I am wondering whether you could reveal the age difference between you and the male job candidate—the one I think you are lying about. I've noticed that feminists tend to look down on age differences in relationships involving a man who is older than the woman. But when the woman is older than the man a strange form of feminist towel-snapping ensues.

At first glance this double standard appears to be discriminatory toward men. But isn't it really sexist towards women? Think about it and write me back.

Update: *The recipient of this letter is an important witness in the aforementioned lawsuit. Therefore, this letter was not sent to her. She'll have to buy the book just like everyone else.*

6

SEEKING MALE PROSTITUTES:
NO EXPERIENCE NEEDED

DEAR ROSEMARY:

It looks like we have a big problem on our hands. It is a problem that, if left unresolved, will drastically impede our ability to increase the percentage of female professors here at UNC-Wilmington.

Recently, a female professor at UNCW was boasting openly about a romantic relationship she had with a job candidate. She also expressed great anger that a fellow feminist showed up at the hotel room of the job candidate—while he was in town for the interview, no less—to compete with her for the man's affections.

At first, this appears to be a simple case of sexual misconduct by two feminists. But I see the situation differently. I think women are the real victims here.

Clearly, if we allow feminists to make brief nocturnal visits to the hotel rooms of male job candidates, there is virtually no chance that a man will ever turn down a job offer from UNCW. It is equally clear that we will be in violation of the Fourteenth Amendment's Equal Protection Clause if we fail to provide the same sexual incentives to female job candidates.

Until now I've tried to resolve this matter by recruiting male professors to offer themselves sexually to our female candidates. So far none have agreed. It could be that they are simply not attracted to the women we interview—most of whom are feminists. Or it could be the case that they simply have morals.

So, today, I'm proposing that the university conduct another job search for male prostitutes who would be willing to entertain our female job candidates during the long and otherwise boring recruitment process. By hiring outside help we could avoid needless conflicts of interest. Under my plan, the men sleeping with the female candidates would not be voting on them when we make a hiring decision.

I know my proposal probably sounds strange to you. Nonetheless, I hope you will avoid any unnecessary moral posturing in the form of prejudging the profession of male prostitution. And if you decide to accept my proposal, I know a couple of feminists who would love to serve on the search committee.

Update: Several letters in this book were addressed to Rosemary. They were not sent in the order in which they appear in the book. The second letter that was sent to her was, like the first one, answered by the human resources director. He was polite and offered his help, but Dr. Adams wanted to hear back from Rosemary. Eventually, he just gave up.

7

I HATE THE MILITARY BUT I LOVE A MAN IN UNIFORM

DEAR ROSEMARY:

I hate to bother you again, but I have one final request concerning changes in our recruitment process. This request comes in response to a comment I heard recently during a recruitment meeting—one that leaves me somewhat confused about the purpose of these faculty searches.

While discussing some potential candidates, a feminist made the remark: "This guy went to West Point. He may be too conservative to teach here."

The anticonservative remark was unsurprising. But it was actually the feminist's next comment that really threw me for a loop: "But, then again," she continued, "I'm really attracted to military guys."

After the meeting, one of the other male faculty members asked rhetorically whether a man could have gotten away with making such an inappropriate remark during faculty recruitment. I stated jokingly that I considered it to be a search for new faculty members, not a search for new husbands. In light of the fact that the feminist's first husband left her for a younger woman, that was probably inappropriate. I'm really sorry about that remark.

But the reason I'm writing you today, Rosemary, is that I've been thinking a lot lately about equality. In fact, since we started this whole diversity thing, I just can't stop thinking about equality. I think about it almost as much as I think about sexual freedom.

So, before I submit my request, I want, first and foremost, to restate my unequivocal support for sexual freedom. This has been the crowning achievement of the feminist movement and I would in no way want to interfere with a feminist's desire to engage in sexual exploration—so long as the object of her affection is a consenting adult.

So, instead of chastising the feminist for using the search committee to find men, I think we should, in the name of equality, of course, allow men the same privilege this feminist seems to think she enjoys. In other words, we should let the male faculty members use the search committee as a way of picking up women. This brings me to my request.

In order to better facilitate matchmaking during the hiring process, I submit that we modify our ads to require job candidates to submit photographs with their other application materials. This will help committee members to better decide whether they are "attracted to" a given applicant.

Also, please recall that in two previous searches we have accidentally interviewed a white candidate mistakenly thinking he was black. Those two mistakes resulted in a loss of thousands of dollars spent interviewing candidates who weren't really "qualified" for the position. Under my plan, we will now know with certainty which job candidates are black—regardless of whether we find them attractive.

Thank you in advance for your kind consideration.

Update: If you're reading this in the bookstore, Rosemary, please take the time to respond. And, please, buy a copy to go with your skinny latte!

8

WHO'S YOUR DADDY?

———————

GOOD MORNING, JAMMIE:

I'm writing you this morning to express my irritation over a remark you made Friday night while we were having dinner at Henri's restaurant on 17th Street. I appreciate your taking the time to organize an outing for the faculty in our department. But I don't appreciate what you said to me while we were having drinks and waiting for the main course to arrive.

I'm not certain whether I was or was not actually staring across the room at the young woman who was tending bar that evening at Henri's. That's my business, not yours. When you said "Stop looking at her, she's young enough to be your daughter," perhaps you thought you were being cute. But I don't like feminists who consider it their responsibility to constantly watch other men to see if they are watching other women.

Nor do I like it when nosy feminists form moral judgments about what they think they have seen a man seeing and then voice that judgment out loud to (or at least try to) embarrass the man. Jammie, I am beginning to think you are suffering from heterophobia.

But before I begin to explore your possible heterophobia, I want to explore your well-established hypocrisy. Shortly after your silly remark, I walked over to the bar to ask that bartender to give me her age—but not her phone number. By the way, she's exactly ten years younger than me, so I guess I'm really not old enough to be her daddy. This brings me directly to the issue of your hypocrisy.

Lately I've noticed that you've been spending a lot of time with another professor in our department who is twenty years older than you—clearly old enough to be your daddy. Since you've expressed your unsolicited opinion, based merely on a possible glance across the room, on the issue of whether a prospective relationship is proper, I figure it's my turn to do the same. My unsolicited advice is enumerated below in five simple points:

First, it is my unsolicited moral judgment that it is inappropriate for you to spend time with the aforementioned professor because he's old enough to be your daddy. A ten-year age difference would be acceptable, but twenty is just ridiculous. That guy was probably dropping acid in the sixties at least two years before you were born.

Second, it is my unsolicited moral judgment that you need to spend more time with your husband. It is important that your young child knows who her father is and who her mother is. That may seem old-fashioned, but, after all, it is unsolicited advice I'm offering. You've never had a problem with unsolicited advice, at least before today.

Third, it is my unsolicited moral judgment that you need to spend more time with your newborn baby. The other day when your husband brought her in the building—because he could not stop her from crying—she disrupted my class, which was meeting just down the hall. You were not in your office, by the way, because you were out walking around campus with the married man who is old enough to be your daddy.

Fourth, it is my unsolicited moral judgment that it was wrong for you to give your newborn baby a hyphenated name. You don't always have to make a feminist statement, you know. I'm also wondering whether you have considered the consequences of hyphenating every baby's name. For example, what if a feminist's child—let's call her Mary Smith-Jones—marries another feminist's child—let's call him John Davis-Johnson. Will their child have the last name Smith-Jones-Davis-Johnson? Where does it all end? At some point, doesn't this become child abuse?

Finally, I just want to remind you that if you critique my potential personal choices in public, I'll do the same to you. I think you should have just minded your own business, especially since you are "pro-choice" and believe in a constitutional Right to Privacy. In your efforts to make a fool out of me, you've made a bigger fool of yourself. Who's your daddy now, Jammie?

Update: *Unfortunately, Jammie responded to an interview request by asking for a two-week period—between completion of any chapters in which her quotes appear and publication date—to review the manuscript in order to remove any "misquotes."*

Unfortunately, Dr. Adams does not give final editorial control to the feminist interviewees. This is a good example of how feminists will not enter into dialogue or debate without being given complete control over the outcome in advance. Also of interest, Jammie's response to Dr. Adams was in all lowercase letters. This is a common feminist practice to decry the "patriarchal" nature of capital letters. They seem to remind many man-hating feminists of an erect penis.

9

JAMMIE'S LYIN'

HELLO, JAMMIE:

As you know, last Saturday was graduation day at UNC-Wilmington. After graduation, when I was out having dinner, I ran into a student who had just graduated. In fact, he took a sociology class under you this past semester.

In the course of our conversation, this student talked a lot about your class. He seemed especially disturbed by a lecture you gave on the topic of tolerance and diversity. He claims that, during the lecture, you told the class about a conference you recently attended with another professor in our department. He also says you claimed to have shared a hotel room with the professor on both of the nights you were at the conference. Then, he says, you revealed to the class that your roommate was a male professor. He says you also told the class that you are both married to other people.

The student concluded his lengthy critique of you and your class by asking me the following question: "What the (expletive) is wrong with that crazy (expletive)?"

Although I strongly disagree with his choice of words, I agree

---

with his assertion that there really is something wrong with you. So I answered his question by providing two possible explanations:

> Your professor is simply arrogant and unethical in the sense that she does not believe that the rules of professional conduct apply to her. The professor with whom she shared a room is a tenured professor who is responsible for observing some of her lectures and evaluating them. Given that these evaluations will be used in her tenure decision, it would constitute a conflict of interest were she actually involved in an extramarital affair with him.

> Or, if she is not actually having an extramarital affair with the other professor, she is simply consumed with anger toward men in general and her husband in particular. When she submitted her receipts to the department secretaries for reimbursement she revealed that she had shared a room with a man to whom she is not married. That really set the rumor mill in motion. And by sharing the story—as a "lesson in tolerance," no less—with the students in her class, she virtually guaranteed that her husband will find out about her sleeping arrangements. It is entirely possible that she's just trying very hard to be as disrespectful and hurtful toward her husband as she possibly can.

So, there you have it, Jammie. I offered the student two explanations for your conduct. If the first one is right, I'm afraid you've committed a breach of ethics that could cost you your job.

But if the other explanation is right, and you are just trying to make it look like you're having an affair, the consequences will be different. You'll get to keep your job but you'll also reveal yourself as a man-hating feminist who is just too ridiculous to tolerate.

To be completely honest with you, I doubt you are having the affair. But I wish you were so we would have an excuse to fire you. The students who are taking your classes are paying serious tuition dollars. But they are being deprived of the opportunity to get a serious education.

So, please, stop waging a war against the male population. As a college professor, you're supposed to be waging a war on ignorance.

Update: Speaking of war, Jammie was caught canceling a week of classes in March of 2003 to protest the war in Iraq. Her students were given extra credit to help her protest the war and antiwar posters were run off (at taxpayers' expense) on the department copy card. Nonetheless, she was given tenure by a unanimous vote just six months later.

10

THE MALICE COWBOY
CHEERLEADERS

Hello, DR. ELLERBY:

I am writing today with a request. Several years ago you were a leader in an organized feminist effort to stop the Dallas Cowboy Cheerleaders from visiting the campus of UNC-Wilmington. As I understand it, campus feminists were offended by the initial invitation of the busty Cowgirls because they felt these underdressed ladies projected a chauvinistic view of what a woman should look like.

During the Cowgirl controversy, some feminists even expressed the view that exposing college women to scantily clad, thin, and busty women would cause a campus-wide epidemic of eating disorders. But by blocking the appearance of the Cowgirls you seem to have saved the day. I've seen little evidence in recent years of anorexia or bulimia at UNCW. Congratulations on a hard-fought victory.

Campus feminists may also have helped to control eating disorders via their sponsorship of Body Image Awareness seminars and annual pageants featuring obese models. I attended one of these pageants and I admire your vision. I know that convincing people that "fat is in"—as opposed to the idea that "thin is in"—is going to be a long and arduous task. I must say that I also admire your patience.

But, recently, while I was strolling around campus, I saw something that bothered me. There were posters hanging all around UNCW that feature a naked man standing up and facing away from the camera. His hands were folded behind him but not in such a way as to fully cover his naked buttocks.

It isn't just his nakedness that bothers me. I am also bothered by the fact that he's so skinny. And, worse than that, the posters of the naked man were adorned with the words "Gender Arts Festival: Sponsored by the Women's Resource Center."

Since you, Dr. Ellerby, are one of the founders of the WRC, I was hoping you could join me in the fight to remove these unseemly posters from our campus. I fear that if we do not act soon, there may be an outbreak of anorexia among the male student population at UNCW.

Please give this matter your serious consideration. And, please, get back to me at your earliest convenience.

Update: Dr. Adams is still waiting to hear back from Dr. Ellerby. He's also waiting for Haley's comet to make a surprise appearance.

II

FAG HAGS AND
RAINBOW FLAGS

Dᴇᴀʀ ᴊᴀᴍᴍɪᴇ:

As I sit here in Port City Java—my favorite coffeehouse in Wilmington—I am admittedly eavesdropping on a conversation taking place at the next table. For the last forty-five minutes a young feminist has been listening to a gay man talk about a variety of problems he's going through. While she's been nodding attentively, she hasn't been able to say much in return.

I know the attentive young lady is a feminist because of her spiked hairdo, horned-rim glasses, and "girls kick 🐴" T-shirt. I know the talkative man is gay, not because of his lisp, but because he's been complaining, among other things, about his gay lover and his job at a local beauty salon. But it's really getting old listening to all his whining.

First off, the man complained about his landlord writing him a citation for hanging the beach towels over the balcony. That took fifteen minutes. Then he started in on his boyfriend's emotional detachment and lack of grooming in recent months. That took about fifteen minutes. For the last fifteen minutes, he's been complaining about his boss at the hair salon. And the nodding feminist just can't seem to get enough of it. I've never seen someone smile so much. If she had a tail, she'd be wagging it back and forth.

Their conversation reminds me of a theory I recently developed on the two types of homophobia. It's a theory that began to take shape when I was celebrating a holiday at a lake house with a bunch of friends. Reactions to the one gay male at the gathering were the true inspiration for my new theory.

One man, Carl, whose girlfriend knew Andrew, the gay man, was a "classic homophobe." When he met Andrew he refused to shake hands as if he would contract AIDS by simply touching him. Fortunately, Carl was outnumbered by "classic nonhomophobes" who simply shook hands with Andrew when they met him and treated him like everyone else throughout the weekend.

But then there were these two feminists at the gathering who could not get enough of Andrew. They followed him everywhere and laughed at everything he said—good jokes as well as bad jokes and even nonjokes. These types of women have traditionally been dubbed "fag hags." Today I am renaming them as "nontraditional homophobes."

The reason I call them homophobes is that they, like the girl next to me in the coffeehouse, will put up with an infinite amount of gay self-absorption—nodding and smiling and saying "that's fabulous!" every few seconds—in order to avoid sending the message that they disapprove of homosexuality or homosexuals in any way. Their zeal to send an "I like gay people" signal is akin to the racist's assertion that "some of (his) best friends are black."

In other words, they have an irrational fear of offending gay people. The reason for this particular form of homophobia is the awareness that gays have a tendency to break down emotionally at the slightest hint of disapproval.

This brings me to you, Jammie. I've noticed that you practically shout across rooms and stand on your chair in the cafeteria to acknowledge every member of the Pride group that comes into your field of vision. You wear a "celebrate diversity" or "gay friendly" pin on your shirt almost daily. You also have a rainbow flag on your office door.

What motivates you—as a straight woman, no less—to try so hard to send an "I like gay people" message? Do you really like them? Or are you just afraid of them? And why is it that every so-called fag hag is also a straight feminist?

Update: Dr. Adams asked Jammie why she makes fun of women with breast implants despite the fact that she encourages men who want to have sex changes. Jammie responded by saying "Our contradictions make us human." Dr. Adams disagrees. He thinks our obsession with homosexuality makes us subhuman.

12

THE INTERROGATION STOPS HERE!

Good morning, Eleanor:

I hope you'll take the time to answer a brief question I have concerning your abrupt exit from one of our department meetings. I am referring, of course, to the meeting that was dedicated exclusively to a discussion of charges of sexual harassment against the chair of the department.

You will recall that we all sat for the better part of an hour listening to a feminist claim she had been harassed by the chair. I started to pose a question to the accuser during the first part of her presentation of evidence. But she asked me—politely, I must admit—to hold my questions to the end. I complied with her request.

However, by the time we reached the end of her presentation, she had accused the chair of harassing three different women. So I decided to ask a question that was very different from the one I started to ask earlier in the hour. You will recall that my question was simply, "Have you ever, in the past, levied a false accusation of sexual harassment?"

I thought the question was reasonable. Apparently, you did not. In fact, you stormed out of the room saying "I will not sit here and listen to a police interrogation!"

In other words, you patiently listened to a fellow feminist destroy a man's reputation for the better part of an hour but blew a fuse when the accuser was asked a simple question. Remember, too, that she had specifically invited people to ask questions following her list of accusations.

At first I was concerned with your angry outburst simply because of what it reveals about your character, or lack thereof. But later I began to consider the practical consequences of allowing women to have an "open microphone," so to speak, for making harassment charges without being subjected to any form of cross-examination or, as you say, "interrogation."

My concern that such a double standard would increase false accusations has since been supported by specific evidence. In fact, as I write this, I am holding a relevant memo from the UNCW Human Resources Department. The memo clears a man of wrongful charges—charges similar to those levied against the chair at the meeting you angrily left. Those charges were levied by the same feminist you defended.

And so, today I write to ask you a simple question: Would you like to see a copy of the memo that proves your shielding of a lying feminist has helped embolden her, even helping her to tarnish another innocent man's reputation?

Or would that induce another outbreak of self-righteous feminist rage?

Update: Eleanor will be a witness in the aforementioned lawsuit. As such, she was not sent this letter. Hopefully, her deposition will not be seen as an unjust "interrogation." If she blows another fuse, she won't be able to simply run out of the room.

13

JUST THE FAX, MA'AM

Dear diane:

I just wanted to drop you a quick line to apologize for my behavior this morning. When I went into the office and was unable to find anyone who could operate the fax machine, I got a little frustrated. Perhaps it wasn't my place to walk into your office and point out that none of the student workers seem to be able to operate any of the standard office equipment.

I was also out of line when I suggested that it was (a) the secretary's responsibility to train the student workers, and (b) your responsibility to reprimand them if they didn't.

As I walked away this morning, you asked the following question: "Why don't you just train the student workers to use the fax machine yourself, Mike?" Now that I've apologized, I'd like to take a moment to answer.

It seems that every time I enter the office, the same three women are deeply engrossed in conversation—one is a professor, one is a secretary, and one is a student worker. It also seems that every time I walk into the office, they abruptly stop talking. For some reason,

I don't feel comfortable just walking over and initiating a facsimile training session.

I don't mean to sound paranoid, but what do you suppose they're talking about in the office for hours on end? And why can't they just share the subject matter with me instead of suddenly hushing up?

Please get back to me as soon as possible.

Update: *It wasn't necessary to send this letter to Diane. Eric, an in-the-closet conservative student worker, provided all the information Dr. Adams was seeking.*

14

THE LIAR, THE WITCH, AND THE WARDROBE

DEAR ERIC:

Thank you so much for your help this afternoon! Lately, I've been a little down on you for keeping your conservatism to yourself—at least while you are in the office. But this time it paid off in a big way.

The three liberal women deeply engrossed in conversation today honestly thought you were studying for a test, which would make sense, given that you are a student worker. Little did they know you were actually taking notes about their conversation—notes you would later share with the department's only conservative professor.

I have a few observations regarding the comments of the feminist professor. Of course, I'm not surprised she's angry with me. Nor am I surprised she decided to criticize me by name in the office. As you know, I criticized her publicly in a recent column for filing a false sexual harassment claim against another professor. But her claims that I am guilty of sexual harassment, merely because I criticized her for the false accusation, are amusing.

Nonetheless, the woman is simply a liar who has been publicly discredited. I think you should just ignore her.

I also have some observations regarding the comments of the

feminist secretary. Don't get me wrong, I do sympathize with her because of her need to accuse her husband of an inability to satisfy her.

The point is that she should not be talking about her husband's ED and complaining that she can't get any good sex anymore while you are within earshot. The feminists should talk about that stuff in the women's bathroom so I can eavesdrop on them.

This secretary is a real man-hating witch, Eric. I think you should seriously consider filing charges of sexual harassment against her. If that's not a hostile environment you're working in, I don't know what is.

Finally, I have some observations about the feminist student worker—the one who never wears a bra to work. She always wears thong underwear though. We know that because her pants are almost always close to falling down. And that's what makes her habit of bragging about her sexual conquests—in the office and in front of you, no less—so problematic.

I don't think I have a right to interfere with her goal of sleeping with every male member of the cast of the television show *One Tree Hill*. Every since they started filming the show here in Wilmington, many young girls have shared the same dream.

It's just her habit of keeping the office informed of her progress that I want to interfere with. Maybe she thinks it's great that she's already had sex with three of them. But the next time I hear her say "three down, four to go" I hope she's talking about the seven letters I recently asked her to fax.

Eric, if this fellow student is going to talk about her sex life, she really needs a new wardrobe. The fact that she talks about such things with her breasts hanging out is a double tragedy. Again, that didn't come out like it was supposed to.

The point is that you need to file a charge of sexual harassment against her, too. If the situation were reversed, I think you know what would happen.

Update: Eric graduated from UNCW without filing sexual harassment charges against anyone. Dr. Adams, though deeply disappointed, still consented to write letters of recommendation for Eric after he decided to come completely out of the closet.

15

CONTRARY TO
PUBIC [*SICK*] OPINION

DEAR DR. DEPAOLO:

Last summer, a memo concerning our "summer dress code," which is in effect every year from May to August, was sent to all faculty and staff. I am writing to request another memo that will offer permanent guidelines to faculty and staff (and students, too) concerning the sensitive issue of nudity in the workplace.

Nudity has been an increasingly visible problem at UNC-Wilmington—one that unnecessarily distracts us from our teaching, research, and service mission. Just recently, in fact, the department secretary asked me to come out in the hall to look at a woman whose breasts were literally falling out of her shirt. I respectfully declined and went straight to my home office to start this memo. Please feel free to pass that information on to my wife.

In addition to the problem of nipple exposure in the workplace, I wanted to write about another more delicate issue; namely, the steady lowering of jean and skirt placement in relation to women's hips. Increasingly, women in our university community are competing with one another to see who can pull her jeans or skirt down the farthest without actually mooning a classmate or coworker.

A few weeks ago a woman who walked into our office made me think the whole competition had gone too far. Had she not carefully shaved that morning, we all would have caught a glimpse of natural body hair even more unsightly than a Frenchwoman playing volleyball in a tank top.

Since things have gotten so bad, I am requesting a memo that makes two points:

1. Women who do not own bras or tight-fitting shirts can avoid unnecessary nipple exposure by wearing Band-Aids. The product is inexpensive and, in fact, can be obtained at the student health center free of charge.
2. Shaving increasing portions of one's bikini area does not shield one from the accusation of having dressed inappropriately. Were it otherwise, the university would have to allow members of the swim team to come to school in a state of complete nudity.

Hopefully, Dr. DePaolo, you will see fit to send such a memo at your earliest convenience. And then, if you have time, you can answer these few questions:

Why is this problem of increasing nudity happening in the wake of a stricter definition of sexual harassment? Why has the nudity gotten so much worse since the school hired its first feminist chancellor? And, finally, now that the feminist movement has our students acting like prostitutes, talking like prostitutes, and dressing like prostitutes, what's next on the feminist agenda? Legalized prostitution?

BEHIND EVERY SUCCESSFUL MAN, THERE'S A FAT STUPID WOMAN

DEAR APPALACHIAN STATE UNIVERSITY WOMEN'S CENTER:

Just a few minutes ago I was watching television when a really clever commercial came on. This woman was talking into the camera (to a reporter the audience could not see) about her recent decision to switch cell-phone plans. She was articulate, intelligent, and, above all, the polar opposite of her husband.

In the background, you could see that her husband was a fat, semiretarded slob whose only reaction to the good news about saving money on the cell-phone plan was to dance around the living room like a blithering idiot. When the camera panned to him and then back to his wife, she was rolling her eyes. She looked to be mortified with embarrassment.

I've seen a lot of these types of commercials on TV lately, but for some reason I've never seen the reverse scenario. Ask yourself when you last saw a commercial featuring a bright, articulate man doing something good for the family, despite the fat, ugly, or, perhaps even drunken wife who serves as a constant source of embarrassment to the overburdened husband.

But that's television for you. There's always a degree of political correctness to ensure that negative portrayals fall on the right groups of people (generally white males), especially in the world of advertising. But at a university things ought to be different. And that's why I'm writing to you today.

I noticed your website has the following statement on its home page:

"Behind every successful man is a surprised woman."
—MARYON PEARSON

Unfortunately for your Women's Center, I also noticed that the university defines this quotation as a form of sexual harassment. Specifically, your school does not allow any speech that suggests a person can perform a certain job or task better or worse because of gender differences. Since you have clearly engaged in sexual harassment, I propose you immediately adopt one of two alternatives:

One: Display the antimale quote only on odd-numbered days, while displaying the following quote on even-numbered days:

"Behind Every Successful Man, There's a Fat Stupid Woman."
—MIKE S. ADAMS

This alternative will present a diversity of viewpoints on gender differences that will avoid endorsing the overall impression that one sex is superior or inferior to the other. You'll spend half the time suggesting men are a burden to women, and half the time suggesting women are a burden to men. Or,

Two: Just take the Pearson quote down immediately.

This alternative will keep you from being sued just in case every man who logs on to your site is not an incompetent, useless, and blithering idiot. I know the odds of that are slim. But, please, be careful. These days, we're living in a very litigious society.

Update: Just two hours and twenty-eight minutes after Dr. Adams notified them that the Pearson quote was a form of sexual harassment—according to the school's official "Equity Office" definition—the ASU Women's Center took it down.

17

HOW TO START AN EIGHTY-YEAR-OLD VIBRATOR

Dear FEMINIST STUDENTS UNITED:

I want to congratulate you on taking the bold, new initiative of establishing the first Orgasm Awareness Festival in the history of the UNC system. This is something to be proud of and you've really shown your pride with the decision to erect a vibrator museum in the middle of the UNC-Chapel Hill campus.

Most feminists, in their understandable zeal to avoid men, are inclined to collect vibrators. But you've taken this a step further by building a monument to remind women that they don't need men as much as they need a good supply of nine-volt batteries.

But perhaps the nine-volt battery isn't all you need to get along without a man. I read one of your flyers that boasted of a 1924 antique vibrator to be showcased in your new vibrator museum. I was wondering whether you could clarify a couple of questions concerning this eighty-plus-year-old vibrator. Admittedly, a few of us have been talking about it at the office for the last several days.

First, could you tell me whether an eighty-year-old vibrator is made of wood? If so, are there any concerns that using a wooden vibrator might be even more irritating than having a man around,

---

especially if the vibrator is not sufficiently polished? And, second, assuming this vibrator predates the widespread use of nine-volt batteries, what the heck makes it vibrate when it isn't used outside in freezing cold weather?

I'm really looking forward to your response. I might even drive up to Chapel Hill for the Orgasm Awareness Festival if I can just get my wife to come with me.

Update: *The mother of the president of Feminist Students United wrote to Dr. Adams's boss (Chancellor Rosemary DePaolo) to accuse him of sexual harassment for writing a letter making fun of her daughter's group. To date, no charges have been filed and he still can't figure out how to start an eighty-year-old vibrator.*

18

NATIONAL ACT-LIKE-
A-FEMINIST DAY

Dear rosemary:

Recently, you made a tremendous effort to attend the annual performance of *The Vagina Monologues* on the campus of UNC-Wilmington. I say "tremendous effort" because you were actually in Richmond, Virginia, that day on business and had to drive about four hours to make sure you were in the audience together with nearly every member of the campus feminist movement.

But, as you now know, this year's performance offended people for a number of reasons. First, the original version of the play features a lesbian feminist getting a thirteen-year-old girl drunk and having sex with her. The play has been changed so that the girl is sixteen years old. Nonetheless, people are still offended.

Second, the play has a skit entitled "Reclaiming [C.U. Next Tuesday]." This skit suggests that women could become more empowered by calling each other "[C.U. Next Tuesdays]" and, thus, removing the stigma associated with the word.

Third, the program guides this year—printed at taxpayers' expense—contained a political statement saying that Iraqi women are now in worse shape than they were before the United States invaded

Iraq and captured Saddam Hussein. Apparently, those running the women's center think a rape room is better than an "imperialist" occupation.

Finally, the organizers of the play sold vagina-shaped lollipops known as "🐱-pops" on campus to promote the event. These unique refreshments were also sold in the lobby of the auditorium on the night of the play. I'm not sure whether you bought one. I hope not.

My purpose in writing you is not to suggest that any of these tasteless forms of free speech should be censored. As you know, I always try to expand rather than contract the marketplace of ideas, no matter how offended I may become. Today is no exception as I propose the establishment of a National Act-Like-a-Feminist Day to be kicked off, of course, here at UNC-Wilmington.

This special day will be characterized by these four activities:

1. Men on campuses across the nation will be encouraged to get at least one sixteen-year-old girl drunk and then have sex with her;
2. Men will be encouraged to refer to all women, even their professors and girlfriends, as "[C. U. Next Tuesday]";
3. Men will wear T-shirts saying "I think gang rape is better for a woman than American Imperialism," and finally;
4. "Penis pops" will be sold at the first annual showing of our new play, entitled *The Penis Monologues*.

Since you were recognized publicly by the Vagina Warriors at this year's showing of *The Vagina Monologues*, we will establish a group of Penis Warriors to recognize you at a showing of *The Penis Monologues*.

I hope, as you read this letter, you will understand why I took the time to write it. The question of what campus life would be like if everyone acted as obnoxious as a campus feminist is worth pondering.

And, certainly, you must also begin to wonder whether these campus feminists are worthy of your constant pandering.

Update: A Baptist preacher, who is also a UNCW alumnus, drove 140 miles from North Raleigh, North Carolina, to meet with Rosemary to express his disappointment with her decision to attend The Vagina Monologues. *After being told he would have a personal meeting with the chancellor, she decided not to show up, opting to send three "representatives" instead. This has caused many to speculate that Rosemary is actually going to hell as a result. Rumors that her husband thinks he is already in hell cannot be confirmed at this time.*

19

🐱-SLAPPED!

Dear Lynne:

I'm afraid I have some very bad news for you. Enclosed is a copy of a letter from William Fleming, director of human resources here at UNCW. The letter summarizes one crucial aspect of the recent investigation of a professor accused of filing a string of false felony (and sexual harassment) charges against three of her colleagues. The letter, which concludes that the felony charges filed against me were false, has now gone into the personnel file of the false accuser.

That would be you: Dr. Lynne L. Snowden.

You will recall that on February 27, I wrote a column criticizing you by name. I did so because you sent an e-mail to all of the faculty members in our department (except for me) suggesting that I had an "obvious contempt" for all women. After a nonfeminist faculty member forwarded your message to me, I responded publicly in my column by making fun of your silly missive.

I was displeased to hear that scores of my readers looked you up on the university website, found your e-mail address, and sent you nasty messages. But I was thrilled when I found out that you went to the chair to complain that I had created a "hostile working environment" by criticizing you and causing you to get those nasty messages. You thought this complaint would be well-received since it was directed toward a Marxist feminist department chair. But things didn't work out quite the way you planned.

When our Marxist feminist chair came to my office, she calmly asked for my account of how the conflict between us first started. She also wanted to know how it had grown to such an intense level.

Dr. Kimberly Cook, our chair, has been researching the issue of false criminal accusations for years. So I started my account of our bad relationship by telling her how you implicated me of first-degree breaking and entering (a felony charge) in great detail. I specifically told her about how you had told the police I had sprayed tear gas in your office. In fact, I told her everything.

And, of course, I told our chair about your false sexual harassment charges against a previous chair. And then I encouraged her to conduct interviews with all the people I mentioned so she could corroborate the details of my accusations against you. But she did something even better.

When she got back to her office, Dr. Cook called Human Resources and asked to speak to Mr. Fleming. Since I had been accused of the tear gas felony four years before (and had never actually been cleared of the charges), he agreed that an investigation was warranted. And what a model investigation it was.

Mr. Fleming interviewed people in the Dean's Office, the Provost's Office, and the UNCW Police Department, and then issued a letter of exoneration.

And, by the way, Human Resources also found corroboration of my accounts of your paranoid activity including, but not limited to, putting your mail in the department's microwave oven to sanitize it—because you thought people were trying to poison you in the wake of the 9/11 attacks.

Your effort to destroy my career has clearly backfired, Lynne. The truth about your mental and moral incompetence to serve as a college professor is now known to all of your superiors. If you weren't a feminist—an opportunistic feminist, I should say—with tenure, you would probably be out of a job. But since that isn't possible, have you considered installing padded walls inside your office? I've heard they're safe, inexpensive, and, even more important, nontoxic.

Update: Dr. Adams is really looking forward to seeing Lynne's sworn testimony in federal court. But the real question is: Who will sanitize the subpoena letter for potentially dangerous toxins?

20

NOT ALL FEMINISTS ARE DOGS

DEAR GEORGIA STATE UNIVERSITY WOMEN'S STUDIES Institute:

I was visiting your website today and noticed that you have a dog on the front page of your site wearing a name tag that says "Susan Talbert." I believe Dr. Talbert is the director of the WSI. I am wondering whether you are aware of the existence of an unfortunate stereotype of feminists; namely, that they are considered by many antifeminists to be "🐈." Sadly, some antifeminists also believe that all feminists are "dogs."

Have you at all considered the possibility that posting the picture of the dog wearing the name of your institute's director has the unfortunate tendency to reinforce those stereotypes? Wouldn't it be a better idea to put a picture of Hillary Clinton on your site? Or do you think it would make much of a difference?

Update: Dr. Adams never heard back from the WSI. As of this writing, they've kept the picture of the dog on the website—name tag and all. Adams did not understand the relationship between dogs and the feminist movement when he wrote this letter. And the reader is probably having a hard time relating it to the theme of Part I of this book. The reader can turn the page now for a full explanation from a feminist and self-described "Queer Theorist."

21

A GERMAN SHEPHERD
IS A WOMAN'S BEST FRIEND

Dear Alice Kuzniar (Professor, University of North Carolina-Chapel Hill):

I recently had the opportunity to read the abstract of your paper entitled "Queer Pets." For years, I've been concerned that feminists in the campus diversity movement would become so antimale that they would actually begin to advocate bestiality in addition to lesbianism.

Although you would disagree with my assertion, I think your recent abstract is beginning to pave the way for bestiality and other unfortunate extensions of the concept of moral relativism, which is so central to the diversity movement. I have reproduced some quotes from your paper that particularly disturb me. I have also added a couple of questions below for your consideration:

> In your paper you contemplate "whether queer now has a quaint ring to it, marking a nostalgia for the 90s, or whether there are still new arenas where queer theory can be productively deployed without retracing worn-out topics of discussion," and propose a very different application at the risk of outright rejection. You also analyze whether "the strict divide between gay

and straight," **has given voice to a range of sexual expressions, "which can be helpful in opening up an investigation of non-normative bonds of affection and intimacy between humans and their closest nonhumans—their pets."**

Your admission that expanding the term "queer" to "include affective attachment to pets could be seen as pushing the concept to the point of meaninglessness" is admirable.

But I am disturbed by your assertion that **"bonding with pets can be deeply intimate and erotic without automatically suggesting sexual relations."**

Your discussion of the work of Ethel Smyth is also disturbing: **"Smyth, a lesbian, was well aware of the queer dimensions of her devotion to her Old English Sheepdogs.** As the example of Smyth announces, the self-consciously queer dimensions of pet love among gay and lesbian writers will be the focus of my paper. In addition, although it would be appropriate to examine the writings on cats by such famous lesbians as Colette and Rita Mae Brown, **I want to limit my study to dogs, largely because the loyal companionship they offer more readily suggests an alternative to normative partnering."**

I agree with this statement:

"The fear of arousing the suspicion of beastiality prevents us from approaching the inordinate affection for pets as a queer topic." But I disagree with your view that this fear needs to be examined. Nor do I join you in lamenting the fact that **"Unfortunately, queasiness—either about the hint of sexuality or, its opposite, sentimentality—has even led to the avoidance of the profoundly serious topic of intimacy with pets."** I nearly lost my breakfast when you said this topic offers a **"provocative new avenue for queer investigation.... I am excited about this new way**

in which queer can let me address my passions! I'm sure many other queer dog lovers at the conference would share them!"

After reading your abstract, I must ask whether you have ever studied under Peter Singer, the Princeton philosopher who refuses to condemn the mutual sexual satisfaction between man and dog, unless the dog is physically injured. I am also left wondering how your position as a professor of German in the Foreign Language Department qualifies you as an expert on "Queer Pet Theory."

Finally, could you tell me what moral basis you have for opposing bestiality? If a feminist is going to avoid men her whole life, she has to leave her options open.

Update: The German professor never responded to Dr. Adams's kind letter. In my imagination she defecated on the carpet when she received it, and her life partner, fortunately, was there to clean up after her. Truly, dog is man's (and lesbian's) best friend after all.

For Further Reading
   Alice Kuzniar. *Melancholia's Dog: Reflections on our Animal Kinship*. Chicago: University of Chicago Press, 2006.
   ———. *The Queer German Cinema*. Palo Alto: Stanford University Press, 2000.

22

SOCIAL WORK
FOR WOMEN ONLY

DEAR KAREN:

Several years ago a student reported that he suffered gender discrimination when he tried to sign up for a class called Women in Social Work. He claimed specifically that the professor said he could not sign up for the class because it was "for women only." Furthermore, he reports that you were the professor in the class.

I was temped to let this matter go, but I'm afraid I can't for two reasons. First, I have since had three more reports—all from men, unsurprisingly—saying you discriminated against them in another class. This other class was not Women in Social Work, so apparently you had to allow everyone in, regardless of their genital structure. But they all claim you discriminated against them in grading after you let them in the class.

Second, I have learned that you were recently promoted to an administrative position. I always enjoy exposing the hypocrisy and antimale bias of feminist professors. But it's even more fun to do the same thing to administrators.

Accordingly, I am asking you to answer the following questions:

1. Is it true that, in the past, you have kept men out of your Women in Social Work class? Before you answer, please understand that I've already researched your accuser's claims and noted that the class he sought to enter was indeed 100 percent female.

2. Just how many times have you been forced by your department chair to change male students' grades? Would multiple instances prove a pattern of discrimination against men?

3. Finally, I'm thinking about posting a sign that says "Criminal Justice for Straight White Men Only" on the doors of all my classes. Do you think I should be fired or instead promoted to an administrative position?

I hope you'll take a few minutes to answer my questions, Karen. If you don't answer them all, I plan to pose them to the provost, the president, and the board of trustees until I get an answer.

Update: Dr. Adams received an out-of-office reply to this e-mail. That was three months prior to this update. Maybe Karen hasn't made it back into the office. Or maybe she can't give a truthful answer without inviting another federal lawsuit.

23

A WOMAN IS INNATELY GOOD AT MATH UNTIL SHE CHANGES HER MIND

Dᴇᴀʀ ʀᴏsᴇᴍᴀʀʏ:

A UNCW student sent me an e-mail discussing his recent interview with you on the topic of free speech. He asked you some specific questions about free speech on our campus. Apparently, you gave some answers with which I disagree. But that's not why I'm writing to you today. Instead, I'm writing about a free speech controversy that occurred on another campus; namely, the one at Harvard University.

When Harvard president Larry Summers suggested that there are innate differences between men and women in math and science ability, the feminists went wild. The following year, he was voted out as president of Harvard University, largely to satisfy a feminist lynch mob. Your remarks to the student who interviewed you indicate your agreement with his dismissal.

This is disturbing, not only because it is an example of feminist intolerance, but because it is also an example of the feminist inability to maintain a consistent position over time. Let me explain.

When I first started to study at the graduate level, I was intimidated by the necessity of taking two courses in statistics, two courses in research methods, and two courses in computer applications.

I was, quite simply, afraid of computers and afraid of inferential statistics.

Nonetheless, I performed extremely well in those classes. In fact, my professor awarded me the first A+ (on a graduate advanced statistics final exam) of his fifteen-year teaching career. So I took an extra statistics class. I also took an extra research methods class and an extra computer applications class.

My proficiency at performing complex statistical analyses on the computer became well known in the department by the time I started my dissertation. In fact, it caused me to be harassed from time to time by students who were not so proficient in dealing with such complexities. One of those students was a feminist.

When she sought my help one night with a statistical technique known as "discriminate analysis," I kindly helped her with a succinct but patient explanation of how best to resolve her problem. But her response made me pledge never to help her again. With a perfectly straight face, she concluded our study session by asking, rhetorically, of course, "You do know that men are innately superior to women when it comes to math and statistics, don't you?"

In other words, she meant to state—as if obviously true—a position that cost Larry Summers his job for even suggesting. But that's not the point. The point, for the time being, is that it offended me.

I had worked very hard to progress in the area of research methods and data analysis. But she simply wrote off my acquired skill as an inevitable consequence of some inborn advantage. I found it as offensive as telling Sammy Davis Jr. that his skill as a tap dancer was due to his inherent rhythm as a black man, which trumped his culturally acquired Jewish-ness.

Of course, it wasn't the first time I had heard such a proposition. It was often said by feminists that the graduate program should be revamped to be less quantitative and analytical in order to avoid an "institutional bias" against females. I dismissed the remarks at the time. But in light of the Larry Summers incident I am beginning to rethink them.

In all likelihood, the offense taken toward the Summers remarks and against Summers himself is an outgrowth of the recent trend in academia toward postmodernism. In the postmodern academic world, the assault on "inherent right" and "inherent wrong" is so aggressive that there is now an assault on "inherent anything." I'll be writing you again in the near future to discuss how this assault relates to cultural Marxism.

But, for the time being, I have a simple request. When you discard an idea you once embraced—perhaps because it is no longer to your advantage—please notify us that you now deem it to be offensive. Let us know that we can no longer express the idea without the prospect of losing our jobs.

One way you might want to keep us informed of such changes would be an actual list distributed at the beginning of every semester letting us know (a) how feminists have changed their minds, and (b) how it could affect our livelihood.

Please note that I am not lending credence to the old stereotype that a woman can't make up her mind. The gay rights activists do it, too. After telling us for years that the word "queer" is offensive, they are now calling their programs "Queer Studies," teaching courses in "Queer Theory," and building "Queer Resource Centers."

Please give my idea about such a list serious consideration. And if you adopt it, please adopt it for good. Don't go changing your mind a few years later.

Update: Dr. DePaolo's constant changing of hairstyles is also evidence that she has trouble making up her mind. Dr. Adams did not write her with that specific observation due to his fear of being charged with sexual hair-assment.

24

HERE I STAND WITH SCISSORS IN HAND

Dear WENDY:

I am writing to issue a formal apology for my recent remarks during a speech at the University of New Hampshire. During the speech I ridiculed your group—the Feminist Action League, or FAL—by claiming you were called the Feminist Action Group (or FAG) until the campus homosexuals got offended. That was pretty tacky of me. I'm really sorry about that.

It also appears that I misrepresented your actions during last year's "Smash Patriarchy" rally at UNH. During the speech, I described your rally as follows: "It was just a night of feminist rage for a bunch of man-hating feminists running around with scissors in their hands."

Fortunately, during the question-and-answer session following my speech, a young lesbian set the record straight. She informed me—in front of a packed auditorium, no less—that the women were actually wearing the scissors on chains around their necks. She also informed me that they were standing still at all times during the rally. It appears that at no point were the feminists actually "running around" as I had suggested.

That makes all the difference in the world and, again, I'm sorry for the confusion. As I reread the following quote from a feminist at your rally—this time imagining her standing still (not running) with the scissors around her neck (not in her hand)—it all starts to seem so normal:

> Ever since I learned to embrace my feminist nature, I found great joy in threatening men's lives, flicking off frat brothers and plotting the patriarchy's death. I hate men because they are men, because I see them for what they are: misogynistic, sexist, oppressive and absurdly pathetic beings who only serve to pollute and contaminate this world with war, abuse, oppression and rape.

Now that I've apologized, I guess I need to get back to contaminating the world with war, abuse, oppression, and rape. Until your allies decide to unhook their scissors and take that first step, I should be safe from the prospect of castration.

Update: Shortly before this letter was written, Wendy changed her e-mail address and phone number, making it impossible to reach her. She did this, I can only assume, because she believed her critics had violent tendencies.

25

I AM WOMAN HEAR ME SCORE

DEAR JANET:

I was somewhat perplexed by remarks you made last year to the student newspaper, *The Seahawk*, concerning the new website RateMyProfessors.com. The site provides an outlet for students to provide anonymous criticism of professors. There are all kinds of problems with the site, but you chose to focus on the fact that students can evaluate professors according to their "hotness" level. In other words, they can note whether they were physically attracted to the professor, not just whether they enjoyed the subject matter of the class.

I was struck by your classification of this "hotness" rating as being somehow "inappropriate." Since you are a postmodern feminist, I cannot really imagine how you engage in moral posturing on any issue. But on this particular matter you are being remarkably hypocritical. I say that because I have read your memoir.

In the memoir you describe in crude detail your first sexual encounter. You talk about your boyfriend ejaculating inside of you. You talk about cleaning blood off the couch afterward. You talk about blood running out of your vagina in the shower afterward. It is, without question, a very graphic and sexually explicit book. And, I am told, it is a book you assign to your students for use in one of your classes.

My questions for you today are really quite simple: Did it ever occur to you that assigning such graphic accounts of your sex life would arouse the men in your class? And, if so, would their arousal be their own fault? Or did you not expect any men to take your classes? And, finally, would you apply a similar standard to a similarly aroused lesbian student?

Before you publicly criticize students for commenting on their professor's looks, I think you need to provide answers to all these questions. I look forward to hearing from you.

Update: Halley's Comet will certainly return before Dr. Adams hears back from Dr. Ellerby. Even if she doesn't respond, Dr. Ellerby has taught us all that it's never a good idea to buy a used couch. In the words of Kelly Rippa, "You don't know where that couch has been."

For Further Reading

Janet Ellerby. *Intimate Reading: The Contemporary Women's Memoir.* Syracuse: Syracuse University Press, 2001.

26

LESBIANS AGAINST RAPE

Dear susan:

Years ago, I became the first professor at UNC-Wilmington to sponsor a fund-raiser in conjunction with the Domestic Violence Shelter and the Rape Crisis Center. I wanted to establish a relationship with those important organizations by sponsoring an event everyone could enjoy. I chose a five-kilometer run and called it the Run Against Rape. That was eleven years ago.

In recent years, however, I've noticed that all of our fund-raisers decrying violence against women have acquired a homosexual theme. For example, this year the Walk a Mile in Her Shoes event will feature scores of fraternity boys walking a mile wearing a pair of women's high-heeled shoes. There's nothing offensive about it. It's just silly that the university can't do anything without some sort of political statement relating to homosexuality.

But the play *The Vagina Monologues*, which you have been sponsoring for years, is offensive. For example, in the original version of the play, there is a scene in which a woman gets a thirteen-year-old girl drunk and has sex with her. That play was used at antirape benefits until the feminists finally realized that adult sex with a thirteen-year-old generally constitutes rape.

So now, in the written versions of the play, the feminists have changed the age of the rape victim to sixteen so she will no longer be a rape victim. But there's one remaining problem; namely, that the adult gets the sixteen-year-old drunk in the play. And that's illegal, not to mention immoral, in every jurisdiction.

I think this problem could be solved by just abandoning *The Vagina Monologues* and going back to a politically neutral five-kilometer run. Besides, there's no point in trying to promote homosexuality, even if you think it might reduce rape. The gay lobby has decided that homosexuality is genetically determined before birth.

Perhaps the feminists are behind the times and don't yet know that promoting homosexuality is futile. It's tough to imagine but I suppose that queerer things have happened.

Update: Dr. Adams addressed two letters to Susan, who still directs the Women's Resource Center. She never responded to the first letter. She did, however, smile pleasantly at Dr. Adams the next time she saw him in the hall at the university. Although he was unsuccessful at starting a dialogue, Dr. Adams considers getting a feminist to smile to be a noteworthy accomplishment.

27

WHEN FEMINISTS CRY
RAPE (REVISITED)

Dear PROFESSOR HOLLOWAY:

I read with great interest an Associated Press article telling of your recent decision to resign from your committee assignments at Duke University. The article states that you were upset by Duke's decision to invite two lacrosse players back to school now that the district attorney has dropped the charges of sexual assault that were previously levied against them.

You are quoted as saying that "The decision by the university to readmit the students, especially just before a critical decision on the case, is a clear use of corporate power, and a breach, I think, of ethical citizenship." You continue by saying that "Despite our judgments about the prosecutor's own lack of principled conduct, it is not ours to become the judge or subvert the process."

While your statements about "corporate power" and "ethical citizenship" are really too vague and esoteric to analyze, your statements about refraining from moral judgment are much clearer. In fact, they shed valuable light on the feminist inability to detect the contradictions inherent in the philosophy of moral relativism held ostensibly by nearly every self-proclaimed feminist "scholar."

Last April, just a month after the alleged incident, you were one of eighty-eight professors who signed an ad in the campus newspaper, which included quotes about racism and sexual assault on campus. Clearly, you immediately took the position that the lacrosse players were guilty of racism and rape. You seemed to take the position that both racism and rape are morally wrong. In other words, you made some very quick and very public moral judgments.

Now we learn that one of the students you do not want readmitted to school did not, according to the statements of the accuser in December, even touch her during the alleged incident. And two factors—that the accuser was constantly changing her story, coupled with the revelation that the district attorney withheld exculpatory DNA evidence—make it very clear that no rape ever occurred.

But, suddenly, you have developed an interest in the presumption of innocence, which you fear may be violated by readmitting the two Duke lacrosse players.

Professor Holloway, even a seventeen-year-old student taking a civics course in high school knows that the presumption of innocence is a concept that only applies to criminal prosecutions. The presumption applies to citizens accused of rape, not lawyers accused of torts or simple violations of the ABA code of ethics.

The idea that the presumption of innocence applies first and foremost to criminal prosecutions is no mere technicality. It is also common sense. Put simply, it is more serious to lose one's liberty than it is to lose one's property or law license.

Since you are an intelligent woman and could have figured all this out on your own some will say that you are blinded by prejudice because the defendants are white and you are black. I disagree.

I think that you are blinded by prejudice because the defendants are men and you are a feminist. I guess I'm just not willing to grant you the presumption of innocence.

Update: *Professor Holloway's response was "Mr. Adams, You have made the error of anticipating that I would have some interest in what you have to say. I do not. K. Holloway."*

28

SEX TOYS FOR TOTS

MISS TAYLOR:

I read with great interest your recent column, entitled "The New Semester Sex Toy Rush"—in the UNC-Greensboro student newspaper. It began as follows:

> I can't name one friend who doesn't buy a sex toy as soon as their [*sic*] financial aid refund check appears. If it's not a sex toy of some sort, it's a porno DVD or a subscription to a triple-X website or lacy lingerie. There is just no other time of the year when cash is more readily available to us poor college kids. We all know that the money is intended for more "appropriate" things like tuition, books, and food, but I think it's safe to say that most of us will risk going hungry later in the semester if we can get off with something new and exciting now.

At first, I was quite put off by your column, especially since I am an economic conservative who has long questioned the need for federally subsidized student loans. But when I read this next paragraph I had to reconsider my position:

I think the need to retain my femininity is something that kept me from accepting my own queerness for a long time. I like and am attracted to (some) butch women, but that doesn't mean I want to be one. Eventually, I came to terms with it and became comfortable being the dominant one in the sack on a regular basis.

Obviously, this shows that the federally subsidized sex toys have helped to accelerate your transition to lesbianism. And I'm all for that for at least three reasons:

1. Now that you are a lesbian who plays with fake (as opposed to real) penises, you are less likely to murder an innocent child through a procedure called abortion, which your opinion page has endorsed for quite some time now.
2. As someone who has often come across as a man-hating feminist in her columns, you will be less likely to inflict emotional damage upon innocent men. The lesbianism should take care of that altogether.
3. Perhaps most important, playing with fake sex organs will impede your ability to spread sexually transmitted diseases to unsuspecting partners—although the physical descriptions of your sex toys (not reprinted in this letter) will call for additional expenditures for items such as latex gloves and antibacterial hand soap.

As excited as I am about your conversion to full-blown lesbianism, I cannot help but think you've had an unfair advantage in coming to terms with your sexuality. While you have access to student loans to help facilitate your desire to play the roll of "the dominant one in the sack," others have not been afforded the same advantage. I am talking, of course, about girls not old enough to attend college.

I think there is a real need to make sure that our future man-hating lesbian feminists convert to lesbianism as soon as possible. I think it is not at all unreasonable to ask that they be educated about sex toys in high school, middle school, and, yes, even grammar school. But, of course, there is the issue of funding, which brings me to the real reason I am writing to you today.

I am starting my own charity, to be called Sex Toys for Tots, which will help provide younger future man-hating lesbian feminists with free sex toys. And, naturally, I need a spokesperson willing to travel to speak with young girls aged five to eighteen—perhaps even showing them how to use sex toys during their own "coming out" process.

So, before I get any deeper into this subject, I have to ask how much you will charge to be our spokesperson. And, if interested, would you like to be paid in cold, hard cash?

Update: Dr. Adams never heard back from Miss Taylor. Rumor has it she was severely injured while shopping for nine-volt batteries at Wal-Mart. Unfortunately, Dr. Adams cannot confirm the specific details of the incident, but he is convinced that she was struck in the head by one of the falling prices. This is yet another adverse consequence brought on by the exploitation of cheap Asian labor.

29

THE SOCIETY FOR CUTTING UP MEN

Dᴇᴀʀ ᴄᴀʀᴏʟɪɴᴀ ᴡᴏᴍᴇɴ'ꜱ ᴄᴇɴᴛᴇʀ:

I have been asked by a group of men at UNC-Chapel Hill to inform you of a possible violation of the university speech code. This code, as you well know, ensures the right of every UNC student to be protected from any speech that might infringe upon his or her constitutional right to feel comfortable and unoffended at all times.

Unfortunately, there is a manuscript in the library—written by Valerie Solanas and entitled the *SCUM* (Society for Cutting Up Men) *Manifesto*—that threatens to infringe upon male students' comfort rights at UNC–CH. Accordingly I am asking the Women's Center to take a leadership role in banning this antimale treatise from the library.

Given your interest in eradicating gender discrimination, I am certain you will be moved to action by simply reading the following excerpts taken directly from the *SCUM Manifesto*:

> Life in this society being, at best, an utter bore and no aspect of society being at all relevant to women, there remains to civic-minded, responsible, thrill-seeking females only to . . .

---

destroy the male sex ... the male is an incomplete female, a walking abortion, aborted at the gene stage.... He is trapped in a twilight zone halfway between humans and apes. To call a man an animal is to flatter him; he's a machine, a walking dildo.... Every man, deep down, knows he's a worthless piece of s#*t.... The company of the lowest female is preferable to his own or that of other men, who serve only to remind him of his repulsiveness.... The male has a negative Midas touch—everything he touches turns to s#*t. The male's inability to relate to anybody or anything makes his life pointless and meaningless....

The healthy, conceited female wants the company of equals whom she can respect and groove on; the male and the sick, insecure, unself-confident male female crave the company of worms.... The lecherous male excited the lustful female; he has to—when the female transcends her body, rises above animalism, the male, whose ego consists of his 🐓, will disappear.

Those 🐱es least embedded in the male "culture," ... who'd sink a shiv into a man's chest or ram an icepick up his 🐴hole as soon as look at him, if they knew they could get away with it, in short, those who, by the standards of our "culture" are SCUM ... these females are cool and relatively cerebral and skirting asexuality.

Every male's deep-seated, secret, most hideous fear is the fear of being discovered to be not a female, but a male, a subhuman animal.

The male likes death—it excites him sexually and, already dead inside, he wants to die.

The male is, by his very nature, a leech, an emotional parasite and, therefore, not ethically entitled to live, as no one has the right to live at someone else's expense.... The elimination of any male is, therefore, a righteous and good act, an act highly beneficial to women as well as an act of mercy....

SCUM can take over the country within a year by systematically 💣ing up the system, selectively destroying property, and murder.

SCUM will kill all men who are not in the Men's Auxiliary of SCUM ... to aid men in this endeavor SCUM will conduct Turd Sessions, at which every male present will give a speech beginning with the sentence: "I am a turd, a lowly, abject turd," then proceed to list all the ways in which he is.... SCUM, then, will consist of recruiters; the elite corps—the hard core activists (the 💣-ups, looters and destroyers) and the elite of the elite— the killers.... SCUM is out to destroy the system, not attain certain rights within it.... SCUM will coolly, furtively, stalk its prey and quietly move in for the kill.

SCUM will keep on destroying, looting, 💣ing-up and killing until the money-work system no longer exists and automation is completely instituted or until enough women cooperate with SCUM to make violence unnecessary to achieve these goals.... Men who are rational, however, won't kick or struggle or raise a distressing fuss, but will just sit back, relax, enjoy the show and ride the waves to their demise.

Update: The CWC never responded to this letter. It can still be found in the UNC-CH library despite the university's claimed opposition to hate speech.

For Further Reading:
Valerie Solanas. SCUM Manifesto, (2nd ed.) Oakland: AK Press, 1968.

PART II

Why Feminists Hate Women Who Don't Kill Children

30

MADAM OVARY

———

DEAR DIANE:

I enjoyed speaking with you this morning about Alfred, my new pet squirrel. As you know, Alfred joined our family after a cat ate his mother for dinner. Since he was so little—in fact, his mother was still nursing him when he died—I had to feed him milk out of an eye dropper just to keep him alive. As long as he is unable to fend for himself, I will keep a close watch over baby Alfred.

I especially want to thank you for sharing your touching story about the squirrel's nest that fell out of a tree in your yard during a hurricane some years ago. According to your story, the nest housed six baby squirrels. After the nest fell from the tree, the mother just grabbed one baby and carried it off, leaving five behind to die. You said it seemed so cruel but then you added, "I guess the mother didn't have a choice."

As you may have guessed, I did not write to rehash this morning's conversation. I want to relate your fallen nest story to another story, one about a feminist who got pregnant six times and had five abortions. It's a true story, by the way, and it's one that leads to a rather obvious question.

———

If the mother squirrel would have been cruel to freely choose to leave five of her six young babies to die, what does that say about the feminist who chose to have five abortions after only six opportunities?

Update: Unfortunately, Dr. Adams sued Diane shortly after this letter was written. He was, therefore, unable to send this letter.

31

A WOMAN'S RIGHT
TO CROSS BURNING

———

DEAR DR. SALLY JACOBSEN:

As a fellow professor, I am shocked that you recently chose to invite students in one of your classes to "express their freedom-of-speech rights" by destroying an antiabortion display on the campus of Northern Kentucky University. After all, the antiabortion display was erected by an NKU pro-life student group with permission from university officials.

In the novel *1984*, George Orwell wrote about a minister of peace who was really a minister of war. As a university professor who tried to claim destruction of others' property as expression that equals free speech, you demonstrate just how prescient Orwell was. Had he written about you, the title "Minister of Liberty" would have been appropriate.

When you were asked about the incident, you said: "Any violence perpetrated against that silly display was minor compared to how I felt when I saw it. Some of my students felt the same way, just outraged."

So, am I to understand that it is because you are so compassionate and tolerant that you feel you have the right to destroy expression that disagrees with your worldview? Have you anything you wish to say in defense of my characterization of you as a common criminal who is simply morally unqualified to teach at the university level?

Update: As a result of her vandalism, Sally was fired from her position as director of the Women's Center. She never wrote Dr. Adams back. So he decided to write her again.

32

I HAD MY BEST
ORGASM THE DAY I BECAME
PROFESSOR EMERITUS

H<small>ELLO AGAIN, SALLY</small>:

I was taking a look at some of the teaching evaluations posted on www.RateMyProfessors.com. I came across the following—mostly from your Women's Writing class. Could you answer a few questions about the student comments below?:

"The topic was supposed to be women's writing which I learned a great deal about, but it took her forever to get into the actual topic. The class was fun even with the sexual humor. She let us have snacks, it was during dinner time. She graded papers so harsh even the writing center told me I would have problems, but tests were a breeze."

"I had Dr. Jacobsen for 2 or 3 classes—she is a nut case. She's flighty and convinced of her own intellectual superiority. She's also the type not to learn her student's names—she actually commented to me once that she didn't have time for that. Also, she says things that seem pretty **** to me. However, I think she's fair with papers and gives a lot of help in test preparation."

"Yeah, she's crazy and she talks about sex but, come on, we all like to get off subject and talk about sex. The tests are open-book and super easy. The upper division classes don't even have tests! Write one paper and you get an A. That is worth listening to her ramble."

"She is crazy. Everything relates to sex or abortion. She talks about her own orgasms. She isn't clear on test reviews or even when she goes over poems in class. She skips all over the place."

"I had this woman for THREE classes, and by the end she still didn't know my name! She spends about half of each one trying to remember some obscure writer's name that has nothing to do with the lesson. Then the tests are multiple choice, open book, & EASY."

"The women [*sic*] relates everything to sex. She gets completly [sic] off track every class period and she is a tough grader. Over all she's nuts; so good luck."

Sally, these are just some of the comments about your teaching but they reflect two pretty consistent themes. First, you seem unconcerned about your students to the point of not even knowing who they are—even the students who take you several semesters in a row. Second, you seem so self-absorbed that you are willing to talk about yourself in even the most intimate of ways, including the details of your sex life and descriptions of your best orgasms.

A few questions might be in order here:

1. Would you say that talking about your better orgasms caused you to be promoted to professor emeritus?
2. Or, did your promotion to professor emeritus cause some of your better orgasms?
3. Finally, did you actually have an orgasm the day you attacked a pro-life display dedicated to the memory of the four thousand babies aborted in America each day?

Update: Sally never responded to this letter either. Although she is no longer the director of the Women's Center, she still talks about her orgasms and her sex life in class. And people still say they sign up for her classes because she's easy.

33

KILL THE FETUS BEFORE IT COMMITS A MURDER

GOOD MORNING, DR. (KIMBERLY J.) COOK:

I just finished reading your book, *Divided Passions*, which purportedly seeks to explore the apparent paradox involved in opposition to abortion and support for the death penalty. In the early pages of the book, you thank the University of Southern Maine Faculty Senate Research Fund for partially subsidizing the book. I bought it for $45 at Barnes & Noble.

I am stunned that you exhausted taxpayer funds to answer such a simple question. Put simply, people simultaneously oppose abortion and support the death penalty because they assume that the fetus hasn't ever killed someone and the murderer has. In other words, the fetus and the murderer should be treated differently because the presumption of innocence that evaporates with a guilty verdict is still in play while the fetus is in the womb. I could have saved the public a lot of money if we had just discussed this over coffee.

Nonetheless, you conducted thirty interviews of people divided into four groups: pro-death penalty, pro-choice; pro-death penalty, pro-life; antideath penalty, pro-choice; and antideath penalty, pro-life in order to probe this deep intellectual issue. You talk about some methodological problems with the interviews in the following paragraph taken from your book:

> Throughout these interviews, I was asked questions by the person I was interviewing. When that occurred I answered her or him honestly or tried to hedge the question as best I could without disrupting the progress of the conversation. Among feminist researchers this is seen as a difficult area for the qualitative interviewer.... [I] followed my own intuition as to what was best for keeping the conversation on course.

Just as I was thinking (perhaps due to men's intuition) that your small sample and obvious interference with the responses of the subjects prevented your results from being applicable to the general population, you stated that "The qualitative data presented in this book should not be viewed as generalizable to the general population."

It was very odd of you to essentially admit that your study is of little use scientifically. It was also odd that you dedicated a book that is clearly written from a pro-abortion perspective to your son. After you state that your son (Greg) "has been the greatest joy, inspiration, and challenge [you've] ever known," you proceed to advance an agenda that gives women a right to kill their children. Perhaps that is a paradox worth studying with public tax dollars.

As put off as I am by the extreme feminist ideology that pervades your writing, I am even more annoyed by the factual errors that litter this book from cover to cover. For example, you state that "For the death penalty to be used ... [t]he prosecutor must prove beyond a reasonable doubt that the defendant committed the murder with the deliberate intention of killing the victim." You wrote this a full eleven years after the Supreme Court gave the green light for executions of those who killed people accidentally in the course of a felony (provided they played a major role in the felony and showed a reckless indifference toward human life).

Furthermore, you state that "Problems with racial disproportionality persist" in the death penalty twenty years after it was reinstated in the *Furman* decision. You point out that 37.7 percent of executions have been of blacks and 56.1 percent of executions have been of whites (over the twenty years immediately preceding publication of your book). What you don't point out is that over 40 percent of the murders were committed by blacks—and less than 50 percent were committed by whites—during that time period. That is simply inexcusable race-baiting.

While your motive of stirring up racial and gender division is very clear, the same cannot be said of your logic. For example, you accuse the Moral Majority of trying to restore "traditional patriarchal morality" to America by (a) restricting access to abortion, (b) establishing prayer in schools, and (c) opposing sex education.

Given that most of the victims of abortion are women, wouldn't it be more accurate to say that restricting access to abortion is *interfering* with the establishment of a patriarchal society? And what does prayer in schools have to do with patriarchal moral oppression? Are you seeking gender-neutral school prayers or would it be better to start these prayers with the sentence "Our Mother, who art in heaven"?

Perhaps you could also explain your remark that "Motherhood" is "not revered as many in the New Right would have us believe"? It is difficult to read your work because of all the strange jabs that are injected into a manuscript that is supposed to be written by an objective social scientist. It is also difficult to understand some of the praise you heap on the Left in America. For example:

The common foundation for supporting legal abortion and opposing the death penalty is a progressive moral order in which the injustices are seen differently—the government is called upon to remedy injustices to women, ethnic minorities, and the poor, rather than expand punishment under state authority.

While this is an honest admission of the Left's obsession with identity politics, you still fail to address the central moral question: How is support for abortion considered a "remedy" of injustices against women and minorities given that (a) most babies that are aborted are female, and (b) over a third of babies aborted are black even though blacks constitute only 13 percent of the population.

And, of course, now would be a good time to remind you that, although, again, whites commit less than half of the murders, most people who are executed are white. But let us not lose sight of the gender issue by interjecting race into the discussion. On page 29, you state:

There appears to be an identifiable punitive element to the restrictive abortion legislation passed in recent years. Women have been targets of punitive control by the traditional patriarchal social order for hundreds of years.

I think at this point you would do well to address two issues. First, you need to answer the question I have raised about female babies being aborted more often than male babies. Second, you need to link this issue to your Marxist ideology. Tell the readers how the atrocities committed against women in our traditional American "patriarchal social order" stack up against the atrocities committed against women in communist societies like China. Please focus your attention on infanticide and the relative treatment of little boys versus little girls.

But, rather than address the obvious moral inconsistency involved in being an anti–death penalty Marxist, you quote "intellectuals" like Granberg who suggest that those who oppose abortion should have "less confidence in the military." The logic of these Leftists is so lacking that it is difficult to offer a rational critique.

As bad as these "intellectuals'" logic can be, it is strong compared to their understanding of basic legal terminology. You quote Durham and associates as saying that some of the respondents in their research would "like to see the death penalty used for a wider variety of murders, such as those involving voluntary manslaughter."

Even the eighteen-year-olds in my freshman survey course are required to know that voluntary manslaughter is not a form of murder. Voluntary manslaughter—or should I say "person slaughter"—is a homicide that is provoked resulting in a negation of deliberation, which, in turn, negates the malice aforethought required to sustain a conviction for murder. Someone with a Ph.D.—and conducting research in the field of criminology—should certainly know better than to make such a fundamental error.

You state on page 61 that research has shown a close association between white racial prejudice and support for the death penalty. But, unfortunately, you fail to report exactly how strong that association is. That is problematic because sociologists have a reputation for using very large samples, which cause any correlation—sometimes even a correlation of less than .1 on a scale of zero to one—to be statistically significant. The sociologist then describes the correlation as "close" or "strong" to the unknowing public.

But, again, this claim of a "close association" makes no sense given that most murders are committed by nonwhites and most people executed (in the last twenty years) are white. This is something you have to address if you are going to succeed in painting whites who happen to support the death penalty as antiblack racists.

Too many pages in your book were squandered by excessive quotation of the subjects of your interviews. Some of these pro-choice subjects' opinions are simply not worth quoting at all. For example, one subject says "I think Rush Limbaugh is a hate monger, like a lot of other people. Like Newt Gingrich and stuff. I totally don't agree with them."

Social scientists should formulate a rule, which says that an interviewee who repeats annoying terms—such as "like," "and stuff," and "totally"—throughout the interview is not worth quoting. They're like totally idiots and stuff. Just ignore them.

But seriously, I wish the following quote from one of your pro-choice subjects was littered with familiar terms—such as "like," "totally," and "and stuff"—because, quite frankly, I can't figure out what the hell she's saying:

> I'm pro-choice and I'm pro-life in the sense that I'm pro-life. I'm for life, I'm for enjoying life. You should be alive, you should be healthy and happy and if I can help you out in doing that, that's great. That's why I don't like it when these pro-lifers are anti-abortionists. So if I were to say to somebody I'm pro-life, they'll automatically assume that I'm anti-abortion. And I'm not. I'm pro-choice. That's why I don't think it's fair they got to use that. You know what I'm saying? It's like it's not fair. Of course, I think everybody should be pro-life. What you do with your body is your own choice. I'm pro-choice."

As I read such quotations, I'm left wondering where you found the subjects for the interviews. Did you stand outside a bar after closing time and just start talking to the drunkest people you could find? I like really want to know because these quotes are just like totally confusing and stuff.

Another of your pro-choice subjects talks about the "Republican conservative orientation people" whose "underlying theory of life is that government should take their hands off." She goes on to say "And yet in their hypocrisy they say that government should put their hands inside my womb, okay? And I'm extremely offended by that."

If I really did want to stick my hands (or the hands of a government official) into the womb of one of your subjects, she should be offended. But, of course, we "Republican conservative orientation people" are only trying to get the forceps, scissors, and suction tubes out of her womb. It's because we respect the privacy of the fetus. In fact, it's one of our underlying values.

But one has to be concerned about the values of some of the pro-choice interviewees you quote later in the book. For example, one pro-choicer describes her decision to abort saying "I did not want to be with my fiancé. I was trying to get away from him." That's interesting. Was she trying to get away from him when she got pregnant? A woman has to be awfully close to a man in order to get pregnant with his child. At least that's what I remember from my high school health classes.

Maria, another pro-choice intellectual giant that you interviewed, says everyone has "a right to their personal beliefs, but [does] not have the right to forcefully and violently impose those beliefs on others." So she's pro-choice and believes she can forcefully and violently impose that view on a fetus?

Another pro-choice interviewee describes a visit to the legislature where she went to testify in favor of abortion rights and, in the process, ran into some pro-lifers. She became angry because the pro-lifer described a newborn baby as "cute." Her response was interesting: "I just wanted to smack her. I wanted to say 'of course, the baby's cute. All babies are cute.' It's like a puppy. Puppies are cute. It doesn't mean we should all have a house full of dogs. I just wanted to smack her."

If I were conducting these interviews, Professor, I would ask the following: "Does your violent disposition cause you to equate children with dogs, or does your view of dogs as equal to children breed (pun intended) your violence?"

But my favorite pro-choice interviewee is Rick, who says that taxing him to pay for "whores and their bastard children really ticks [him] off." So Rick says, "I think they ought to take them all outside and shoot them. I know that's hard core, but by God I'm tired of paying people to have babies when they can't afford to have them." Now, what was that you were saying about pro-lifers being more punitive than pro-choicers?

But no matter how silly the remarks of the pro-choicers, you cannot bring yourself to criticize them. Indeed, you often heap praise where it is quite unexpected. For example, pro-choicer Bob says "People like Pat Buchanan and Bob Dorman scare the hell out of me." There's nothing particularly insightful about that statement. Nonetheless, you respond by saying "Bob is extraordinarily logical in his opinions and very well informed about sociopolitical issues and their histories."

But things are a little different when a pro-lifer, for example, Glen, makes a statement like this: "If you want to deal with the individuals that are making a living by working in abortion clinics, I see them as no different than maybe soldiers that Hitler had ... walking into the concentration camps and guarding so that no one escapes." You then call his statement "extreme." But why is it "extreme"? Hitler killed six million innocent Jews. The feminists have killed fifty million innocent babies. Is Glen's not a logical and well-informed observation about a sociopolitical issue and its history? If not, why?

Toward the end of this book, you step up your attacks on pro-lifers by saying that opponents of capital punishment are "generally more well-informed than the supporters," and that the facts "are on the side of death penalty opponents." Unfortunately, in the same sentence, you repeat the false assertion that the death penalty remains "racially biased" against people of color.

This willful ignorance renders your harsh assertion that a "plurality of ignorance" is responsible for leading pro-life death penalty supporters to "search out information to confirm their opinions rather than allow information to sway their opinions" both ineffective and hypocritical. You lack the objectivity necessary to criticize your subjects for a lack of objectivity.

In the book's final pages, you elevate hypocrisy to a Zen art by comparing pro-life death penalty supporters with the authoritarian personalities studied by Theodor Adorno in the aftermath of the Holocaust. You note correctly that he and his colleagues were "interested in the psychological foundations of prejudice that grew to genocidal proportions during the 1940s." But you are wrong to hint that we must monitor the pro-life death penalty supporters to ensure that their prejudice does not grow to genocidal proportions.

Put simply, we are already experiencing genocide in America. It is being led by pro-choicers like you who are silent about the racism that flows from their agenda—foolishly describing themselves as merely having a "deep commitment to gender equality" and fighting to succeed in the "male-dominated political arena."

While I do not support your "right to choose," I do support your First Amendment right to publish a 203-page opinion piece on the topic of abortion and capital punishment. But it is only an opinion piece, not a scholarly effort. And it certainly isn't objective science.

Update: On advice of legal counsel, this letter was never sent. Flip ahead to "The Sound of Silence" in Part IV to find out why.

For Further Reading:

Kimberly J. Cook. *Divided Passions: Public Opinions on Abortion and the Death Penalty.* Boston: Northeastern University Press, 1998.

34

THE FAULL OF THE
THIRD REICH

Dear David (French):

I am writing today to ask a special favor of you. I need you to take a few minutes to write a letter—one I hope you'll call "Slander for Dummies"—to Katherine Faull, director of the Women's and Gender Studies Department (WGS) at Bucknell University. Dr. Faull is threatening to sue an undergraduate student because she is presently under the impression that forwarding an e-mail—one actually written by Dr. Faull—constitutes slander (because she did not give the student written permission to forward the e-mail). Let me provide you with some brief background information.

A Bucknell student whom I will refer to as Dominic—because that's his real name—wrote a letter to Dr. Faull asking her to sponsor a speech by conservative author Christina Hoff Sommers. When Faull refused to help fund the Sommers visit, Dominic invited her to cosponsor without contributing any funds. Faull refused and even cited the objections of several WGS program committee members who questioned the integrity of Sommers's work. This is really where the trouble began.

After I talked to Dominic, and did some additional research on the situation, I learned that the WGS had sponsored visits to Bucknell by prostitutes, porn stars, and strippers. I thought it was funny that the WGS thought prostitutes, porn stars, and strippers should be funded but conservatives should not—all because of concerns over "integrity."

So I decided to write a column criticizing Dr. Faull for being a narrow-minded hypocrite. She didn't like that. And she also claimed that a portion of my column—saying that Faull was director of the WGS—was false. This claim was made in an e-mail to Dominic. After I found out she was apparently lying—indeed, the Bucknell website lists her as director of the WGS—I wrote another column critical of her dishonesty.

That's when she decided to threaten Dominic with a slander lawsuit for forwarding her e-mails without permission, some of which were reprinted in my column. I don't know how this feminist formed the impression that someone could slander someone else without lying about them. In fact, the only person who apparently lied about Dr. Faull, was Dr. Faull when she claimed not to be the WGS director.

Since you have a law degree from Harvard, David, I'm asking you for this favor: Could you please write to Dr. Faull and slowly explain to her that forwarding an e-mail does not constitute slander, especially when the e-mail was, in fact, written by the potential plaintiff rather than the defendant?

Thanks in advance for your consideration. And, please, David, don't use any big words. These feminists are quite emotional and rather easily confused.

Update: David French responded to the author's letter immediately. He gave his full assurance that clicking on a "forward" button, while sitting in front of one's computer in total silence, cannot constitute "slander."

35

PLANNED CENSORSHIP
AT THE WRC

Dᴇᴀʀ sᴜsᴀɴ:

I recently finished a brief and informal survey of twelve women's centers located across the nation. I called each one in an effort to find a single women's center employee who describes herself as "pro-life."

Unfortunately, of the 120 employees at the twelve women's centers, I was unable to find a single person who subscribes to the pro-life position. I write to you today as I renew my efforts to find some degree of ideological diversity within at least one of these centers.

By looking at your web page, I see that you and Melissa Ennis are listed as "office staff." I also see that Donna King, Amy Kirschke, Vibica Olsen, John Rice, and Kindra Steenerson are research collaborators in the area of "Gender of Art." Adrian Sherman and Ashley Barefoot are listed as collaborators in the area of "International Women's Studies." Javier Gontier and Monica Mackie are listed as collaborators in the area of "Gender, Cohort, and Alcohol." Finally, Carol Prescott is listed as a collaborator in the area of "Race, Ethnicity, and Beliefs about Alcohol."

By my count, there are twelve individuals currently affiliated, either as staffers or researchers, with the women's center. Can you tell me whether any of these twelve are "pro-lifers"?

Update: *Dr. Susan Bullers did not respond to this letter. She is a Democrat who was chosen to be director of the Women's Resource Center by a committee of six Democrats who were replacing the Democrat who replaced another Democrat who replaced the Democrat who was the original WRC director. Dr. Adams firmly believes that the process of selecting WRC directors, staffers, and researchers would be more democratic if it weren't so Democratic.*

36

PLANNED CENSORSHIP
(REVISITED)

Hello again, David:

I'm sorry to bother you twice in the same week but the feminists are up to their old tricks with the Women's Resource Center website. I've written to WRC director Susan Bullers to, or at least try to, establish some sort of dialogue. She won't return my e-mails.

This business of not returning my e-mails is irritating because Bullers's salary is paid by taxpayers like me. It is doubly irritating because I assume a part of Bullers's job description is having to put up with public criticism of the WRC. Bullers probably got sympathy from the administration, at least in part, because she will have to answer a lot of e-mails generated by my columns. She took the money, but now she's refusing to answer the e-mails.

But, of course, I didn't write to accuse Bullers of fraud. I wrote to accuse her of violating the First Amendment by allowing Planned Parenthood to advertise on the WRC website. That doesn't sound like a First Amendment violation until you review the history of their relationship with the proabortion organization.

When the WRC first began to post Planned Parenthood's address and phone number on the site, I personally contacted the center to ask them to put a local Crisis Pregnancy Center (CPC) up there, too. I just wanted women to have a "right to choose" from more than one abortion counseling service.

Unfortunately, the administrator lied to me, saying that there was a policy of "nonduplication," which meant that only one counseling service could be recommended by the WRC. To suggest that a CPC would "duplicate" Planned Parenthood's advice is laughable. Furthermore, the site had two distinct places where a woman could go for counseling after being raped, proving the administrator to be a very bad liar.

When a new director took charge of the WRC, I tried again. This time, the CPC was rejected as a candidate for inclusion on the site because it was "overtly religious." This also proved to be a lie as the university allowed links to a gay website—one loaded with religious information—to be included on the WRC website. The ads for gay churches were placed alongside an essay called "Jesus on a Rainbow," which was all about how Jesus supports the gay rights movement.

So, eventually, the WRC took down the Planned Parenthood information—largely because they knew I was organizing a federal lawsuit against them. That was sad because my goal was never to cut down on a woman's options. I wanted to expand them. Indeed, I always enter free speech controversies with the goal of expanding the marketplace of ideas.

But the feminists preferred having no information on abortion counseling to the alternative of having a CPC included. At least, that seemed to be their stance. But now we see that they really intended to sneak the proabortion information up when no one was looking. And this is where I need your help.

David, I need you to write these women a letter explaining that their postmodern legal theories are unlikely to keep them from losing a federal lawsuit. They are all excited about "feelings" and "perceptions" and probably think that if a tree falls in the forest and no one sees it then it really didn't fall. Similar thinking would lead to the conclusion that if a feminist violates the Constitution and no one notices, the Constitution really hasn't been violated.

But, of course, David, I have noticed what the feminists have done. And I plan to sue. So, please, write soon and explain to them the error of their ways. And remember to speak slowly. These feminists take years to educate.

P.S. In the event that I've made an error in my First Amendment reasoning can we instead sue Bullers for fraud? I think she should pay back that bonus by performing community service at a local CPC.

Update: David French wrote back to tell Dr. Adams that his fraud case was weak at best. And with the help of feminist censorship four thousand babies are still slaughtered in America every day.

37

I WISH YOU WERE ABORTED

Dᴇᴀʀ ᴀɴᴏɴʏᴍᴏᴜs ғᴇᴍɪɴɪsᴛ:

First of all, I want to thank you for attending my recent speech at Wake Forest University. During the question-and-answer session you asked the following:

1. Why do you have to be so caustic and confrontational in your exercise of free speech?
2. Why can't you just sit down and talk with college administrators instead of embarrassing them in the national media?

I already answered the second question by assuring you of three points: First, I always try to talk to college administrators about free speech issues; second, they always ignore me; and third, bad press always gets their attention.

I also tried to answer your first question by asking you to give me an example of "caustic" or "confrontation" speech that I have used in the past. It was really an awkward few minutes as I paced back and forth across the stage waiting for an example of specific speech that offends you while you stuttered, stammered, and, ultimately, provided no example.

Since you seemed so tongue-tied I thought I would write today to give you an example of speech I consider "caustic" and "confrontational" in the hopes that it will refresh your memory. The example I provide below is true and took place only a few days ago.

As I was sitting in my office with my door partially open, I heard someone come to the door and start reading a bumper sticker that says "One out of every four babies dies over choice." It was a feminist so I tried to ignore the interruption and just go back to work.

Unfortunately, the feminist decided to add the following after repeating the line on the bumper sticker: "Too bad one of them wasn't you."

So, do you think it is wrong for a feminist to say, in effect, "I wish you were aborted" to someone who chooses not to be pro-choice? And what was it you were saying to me about "caustic" and "confrontational" speech?

Update: Dr. Adams still does not know who that woman was. But since she attended his speech, he hopes that she's also reading this book. Hence, the next letter you are about to read.

38

SORRY SEEMS TO BE THE HARDEST WORD

Dear anonymous feminist:

I regret that my efforts to find you have been unsuccessful to date. I'm still interested in hearing an example of the "caustic" or "confrontational" language you think I need to stop using in my exercise of free speech. I was also hoping to hear from you about the feminist who suggested my mother should have aborted me. Specifically, I hoped you would muster the courage to criticize a feminist for being overly "caustic" and "confrontational."

Fortunately, since I last wrote to you, there has been a dramatic development in my relationship with the feminist who said he wanted me aborted. Believe it or not, he actually apologized for his remarks.

This marks the first time I have ever received an apology from a feminist. Not even the feminist who was caught filing a false police report against me would offer an apology. She just got angrier with me after I caught her lying.

It is interesting, though, that my first apology ever from a feminist comes from a male feminist, given that there are obviously more female than male feminists. That may be explained by something I've noticed about female feminists over the years.

Generally speaking, when a female feminist gets mad at a man she doesn't tell him why she's mad. She just starts a whispering campaign against the man with no intention of ever confronting him about the issue that bothers her. By contrast, take note of the male feminist who came by my office the other day. He let me know exactly why he was upset with me. And he did it to my face.

Perhaps I should not be surprised that he also walked up to me confidently in the hall the other day to offer an unequivocal apology. He even called his actions "stupid." He sounded just as aggressive in his apology as he did in his insult.

I am wondering whether there are female feminists out there who are sorry for the extreme and hurtful things they say to people in the name of feminism. Is it possible that the same cowardice that keeps them from confronting men they feel have wronged them also keeps them from confronting (with an apology) the men they know they have wronged?

And, finally, after you interrupted my question-and-answer session—with personal criticism you cannot support with any evidence—don't you think you owe me an apology?

Update: *If any feminists reading this want to apologize in writing, my address is: DrAdams.org, P.O. Box 319, Wrightsville Beach, NC, 28480. If your package or envelope is ticking it will be immediately discarded.*

39

I'D RATHER DIE THAN TAKE
CARE OF MOMMA

Dear Ms. (Jenny) Murray:

I am writing you this August afternoon wondering whether the news I just heard about your recent suicide pact is the product of a hallucination. I've been out in the heat all afternoon and I hope I'm merely imagining that you said you do not want to be "trapped" into caring for your sick mother if you also become ill.

Since you are the feminist host of BBC Radio's "Woman's Hour," I suspect that what I'm hearing is true. In fact, I just saw some publicity material for a BBC television show on which you recently appeared—I did not see the actual broadcast—that says you plan to end your own life when you become a "burden" to those around you.

As disturbing as that is, I am even more bothered by BBC's statement that you are "angry that, having fought so hard to become liberated and independent, women are now being trapped into caring for dependent parents."

You have also been quoted as saying that laws against assisted suicide are the product of an outdated moral view that human life is inherently valuable and that children have a legitimate obligation to care for elderly parents.

I hope you will take time out of your busy schedule at the BBC to verify the statements that have been attributed to you. I have long considered the feminist obsession with abortion to be dangerous. I fear that the ability to rationalize abortion can translate into an ability to rationalize just about anything. That's why I seek verification of your remarks.

Also, if you have a few moments I would appreciate your insights into the following question: Does the feminist's hatred of her unborn child cause her to hate her parents? Or does her hatred of her parents cause her to hate her unborn child?

Update: *So far, no response from the BBC feminist. But, thankfully, she hasn't yet killed herself.*

40

SHE'S INTOLERANT? LET'S KILL THE FAT, UGLY 🐱!

D<small>EAR</small> A<small>NDREA</small> J<small>ONES</small>:

I'm writing to congratulate you on what may be the worst piece of journalism I have ever seen from a leftist feminist. I am referring, of course, to your recent article in the *Atlanta Journal-Constitution*.

Your article suggests that a recent victory in federal court—by two traditional, conservative female students at Georgia Tech—amounts to nothing more than a victory for those seeking the right to insult feminists and gays on the Georgia Tech campus.

While I am convinced that you lied in your article just to defame these two students—in other words, you willfully concealed facts you already knew—I want to make absolutely sure that you do know the facts about how this suit came about.

One of the plaintiffs in this federal lawsuit was upset by the tasteless feminist play *The Vagina Monologues*, and decided to criticize it by printing up posters and setting up a booth on campus. When she did, some feminists working for the university made her mark out some comments the feminists deemed "offensive" and "derogatory" toward them. This is where Georgia Tech's unconstitutional speech code comes into play.

The Tech feminist employees who asked the plaintiff to erase certain remarks on the poster board that were deemed "offensive" were engaging in unconstitutional viewpoint discrimination. Obviously, if the feminists are allowed to put on a play with the word "vagina" in it—and parade around stage chanting that word and others too obscene to reprint—then offended students have a right to criticize them for it. Put simply, the Constitution protects feminists and antifeminists alike.

But because the university feminists applied the code selectively—to ban speech with which the feminists disagreed—the antifeminists sued. And they won.

Now, as a result of the suit, the aforementioned speech code has been struck down and Georgia Tech has been placed under court supervision for five years. They cannot develop any new speech codes or student conduct codes without permission from a federal judge.

While your smug column suggested the plaintiffs wanted the speech code abolished so they could insult people, it omitted some important facts about the gay activists and feminists who fought the lawsuit tooth and nail.

You didn't mention the fact that the aforementioned students passed out Hostess Twinkies in the dorm at Georgia Tech while calling the Asian plaintiff a "Twinkie ⬛"—this was to suggest she is yellow on the outside and white on the inside.

Nor did you talk about the leftist gay activists who called her a "fat, ugly ⬛" on the Internet using the university e-mail system. And you omitted any references to the liberals who said—on the Internet, no less—they would like to throw acid in the face of the plaintiff in retaliation for the lawsuit. Finally, you failed to mention the doctored photographs they circulated on the Internet showing the plaintiffs adorned with swastikas.

Instead, you simply sided with a bunch of hysterical racist gay activists because you could not bring yourself to side with traditional women who would dare to criticize feminism. That you did this ostensibly to take a stand against personal insult renders you a very bad liar. Not to mention an equally bad journalist and human being.

Update: Dr. Adams heard back from Andrea just a few minutes after writing her. Missing the point entirely, she characterized his letter to her as "hate mail." She also noted that she wrote another article on the subject, which was kinder to the plaintiffs. Nonetheless, the original piece remains one of the worst articles in American history (in my completely objective opinion).

41

WOMEN WHO GET
MARRIED ARE STUPID

Dear donna:

A couple of semesters ago, I overheard a comment you made about marriage. I wasn't eavesdropping this time. The door to your classroom was open and you said the following in a loud voice: "Now I know you're going to think I'm crazy, but studies prove that marriage is a better deal for men than it is for women."

Could you direct me to the studies upon which you based your lecture? I would like to incorporate them into my new book about feminism.

Thanks in advance.

Update: Unsurprisingly, Donna never provided me the full reference for the "studies" quoted in her lecture. While she did offer a guess that the author of one of the studies may have been "Bernard," she did not know (a) the title of the article, or (b) the name of the journal in which it appeared. Instead, she provided the name of another feminist who is "more of an expert" in the area of marriage.

Please remember Donna's lame response when your eighteen-year-old

---

daughter or sister comes back from college saying her sociology teacher told her that "they" have proven that marriage is an oppressive, patriarchal institution. Make sure you respond by saying that "they" have done studies showing that feminists are too lazy to read the studies "they" use as the basis of "their" antimarriage lectures.

42

"GENOCIDE AWARENESS" DAY

Dear Dr. Minor:

I am interested in working together with the Office of Campus Diversity to bring a new event to UNCW's African American History Month, which was previously known as "February." The event that I envision is a "genocide awareness" day that will help educate members of our university community about the destructive effects the feminist movement is having on the African American community in this country.

The centerpiece of the event would be a display in the University Commons that would be comprised of one cross for every one million babies aborted in America since 1973. I estimate that would require about fifty-one crosses by the time we organize this event. I would like to see thirty-four of these crosses painted white and seventeen painted black. This would be a creative way to show that one out of every three babies aborted in America is black, despite the fact that blacks comprise less than 13 percent of the population.

I would also like to request funding for conservative author Dan Flynn to come to campus to talk about the racism of Margaret Sanger, the founder of Planned Parenthood. This would increase diversity by having a white man speak during African American History Month—we need the integration badly. It would also be a good way to fight the antimilitary bias at our school—given that Dan Flynn is a Marine.

Please give my idea your careful consideration. And let me know what you decide.

Update: Dr. Adams actually heard back from Dr. Minor. The student pro-life group is now negotiating with the Office of Campus Diversity to establish a first annual Genocide Awareness Day. Other groups in Michigan have heard about Dr. Adams's idea, which, after the publication of this book, could become a national event.

PART III

Why Feminists Hate Republicans Who Carry Guns

43

DON'T LEAVE ME TO FESTER IN A POOL OF MY OWN BLOOD

———

Dear anonymous feminist blogger:

Perhaps I owe you an apology for my recent comments about abortion. I stated publicly that there should be a compromise between pro-lifers and pro-choicers in this country taking the form of a six-month abortion season. All abortions would take place between March 30 and September 30. The rest of the year would be abortion free.

I also suggested that women who support abortion should wear orange vests and caps during abortion season to warn men who do not want their babies killed in the event of an unwanted pregnancy. You responded with the following:

> For comments like that, somebody ouaght [sic] to beat the ever loving s#*t out of Mr. [sic] Adams. Seriously. Beat some sense into the mother⬤er. Just kick the s#*t out of him until he's within an inch of his life and then leave him to fester in a pool of his own blood.

Obviously, you misunderstood the point of my commentary. It was clearly directed toward those women who (a) criticize men for hunting (bird-hunting in this particular commentary), and (b) support aborting unborn babies.

When I suggested that it was simply perverse to consider the killing of a quail to be more reprehensible morally than killing an unborn child, you suggested that I should be beaten within an inch of my life and then left to die slowly in a pool of my own blood. This causes me to seek some clarity regarding your position on guns and hunting.

Previously, all of the feminist antigun commentary I've encountered led me to believe feminist opposition to guns is twofold: First, guns cause more people to be hurt accidentally. Second, guns increase the efficiency of those who desire to hurt others intentionally.

But after reading your comments, I am led to believe that you would consider shooting me to be too quick and humane a method of extermination. I want to know whether you really mean to kill me and whether you mean to do so in the most painful manner possible. I also need an excuse to buy another gun.

Update: The unarmed feminist never responded to this short letter. Dr. Adams is yet to be beaten and left to die, festering in a pool of his own blood. He bought a 9mm Glock to celebrate this violent feminist's nonresponse.

44

THE FEAR OF QUEERS AND FEMALE ENGINEERS

DEAR GEORGIA TECH WOMEN'S CENTER:

I write to you today with grave concern about the level of crime, particularly serious violent crime, which seems to have exploded in recent years on the Georgia Tech campus. My concern was raised by some articles I read in the Georgia Tech student newspaper. For example, I read the following:

> "The number of robbery incidents, however, has raised concerns on campus. The string of thefts started early in summer; GTPD had a busy day May 29 with two robberies on opposite sides of campus."

> "In the past month and a half, there have [*sic*] been an increase in armed robberies on Georgia Tech's campus, with three reported since the last week of May."

> "(I)n 2002 crime increased across the board."

"Two suspects robbed at gunpoint two Tech students who were walking back to their East Campus residence hall last Wednesday night, April 7.... [O]ne suspect demanded they produce money 'or I'm going to bust your ⬛.' One of the suspects pulled a silver-color pistol from his waistband."

"A male Tech student was robbed at knifepoint ... at approximately 2 a.m. March 12."

"Fall semester is only a few weeks old, but in that short time there have been a high number of crimes committed on and around Tech campus. The majority of these crimes have involved theft of valuables from cars, cars themselves, and theft of bicycles. However, the greatest area of concern is the dramatic increase in the number of armed robberies in the past few weeks."

"Since August 1, 1988 thefts have been performed on campus. Of these thefts, 105 targeted motor vehicles and their contents and 33 were bicycles."

"In a recent *USA Today* survey, Georgia Tech found itself highly ranked in the company of Stanford, Yale, Duke and Emory. This ranking, however, was not about academics, but crime on campus.... Based on the crime survey, Tech initially ranked No. 2 in the country.... "

"Since the beginning of the semester, there have been a reported 168 thefts, 29 burglaries, 24 counts of trespassing, 105 car-related crimes, 15 DUI's, 41 counts of vandalism, 3 armed robberies, 3 counts of drug possession, 3 counts of underage drinking, 5 frauds, 1 count of sexual assault, and 2 terroristic threats."

Given the rather dramatic incidence of crime on the campus, it is important that measures are taken to protect all students at Georgia Tech. However, to my knowledge, the only significant undertaking in this regard is the proposal for a new Georgia Tech "Queer Resource Center." While this proposed center would undoubtedly provide a "safe space" for "queers," I am concerned that people who are not "queers" will be left in a continued state of vulnerability.

So, today, I am proposing a special initiative at Georgia Tech that will help to protect another potentially vulnerable group at Tech; namely, female students. Best of all, the program will be provided at no cost to the Georgia Tech administration.

For the first phase of the program, I am offering to give a speech at Georgia Tech, free of charge, on the topic of Women and Guns. The speech will endeavor to answer the following basic questions for women who are fearful of experiencing robbery, rape, and other violent crimes at Georgia Tech:

1. What are the basic elements of the law of self-defense? When may I lawfully employ deadly force?
2. How do I obtain a handgun permit in Georgia? What are the best handguns for women to buy?
3. How do I obtain a concealed weapons permit? What are the best weapons for that purpose?

Since I will be speaking at Emory Law School early next semester, I am hoping we can arrange a time for me to give my free speech for the benefit of Georgia Tech women. After the speech, I intend to collect a list of interested women so I can make arrangements for some of my friends in Atlanta to provide some basic firearms training.

Furthermore, if the interest is sufficient, I plan to do some fundraising to help these Georgia Tech women pay for their concealed weapons permits and, if possible, actually buy some handguns for these concerned students. If you will just allow me to come to Tech to speak, we can do something about the recent outbreak of crime at your institution of higher learning.

I envision a day when thugs no longer demand that female students produce money under the threat of getting their " 🐴 busted." I envision a day when the thug is looking down the barrel of the woman's gun and hearing the words:

"I'm not a libber, and I'm not even gay; but if you touch my purse, then I'll blow you away."

Update: The Georgia Tech Women's Center declined Dr. Adams's offer to give a free speech. This goes to show that Georgia Tech is adamantly opposed to free speech.

45

THE RAPE OF BAMBI

D EAR LINDA KALOF, AMY FITZGERALD, AND LORI BARALT:

I just finished reading your article "Animals, Women, and Weapons" in the "scholarly" journal *Society & Animals: Journal of Human-Animal Studies*. While I was captivated by your intellectual prowess throughout the article, the assertion that "sex long has been tethered to hunting in human culture" is the one line that caught my eye and led me to read the entire article.

I've been a hunter now for seven years and was unaware that there is a "Well-established theoretical tradition of connecting hunting with sex" in the "scholarly" feminist literature. Nor was I aware that "The language of hunting is a discourse of patriarchy" and that hunting "Exacerbate(s) male dominance and power." In fact, the last time I went hunting, the largest deer in our group was harvested by a good friend's wife.

While the three of you are undoubtedly my intellectual superiors, I want to caution against making overly confident statements like: "Feminist theory has been particularly articulate in noting the connections between hunting, sex, women, and animals." Let your readers decide whether or not feminist theorists are articulate.

I also want to caution against the following overgeneralization in your article: "Finding sexual pleasure in dominating and destroying living organisms is a 'normal part of men's fulfillment.'" I know you were quoting another feminist scholar when you said that but, please, let's not lump hunters like myself together with homosexuals and metrosexuals who are afraid of the sight of blood.

I noticed that your "scholarly research" was based on the reading of fifteen bow-hunting magazines—I will just assume that each author read five magazines apiece. While that certainly qualifies you as hunting experts in feminist circles, I hope you will not take offense at a small correction offered by someone who reads about fifteen hunting magazines per month—usually without the help of a couple of friends.

In your "research" you stated that "animals were sexualized" with phrases like "hot-to-trot teenage bucks." This was a part of your general assertion that hunting is symbolic of the rape and degradation of women. However, in your research into hunting, you do not seem to have come to an understanding of some basic hunting terminology. For example, "buck" is a term for a male deer, not a female. We call those "does."

These basic terms are important because you expound on the male dominance theme further with the statements: "Violence against animals and women is linked by a theory of 'overlapping but absent referents' that institutionalizes patriarchal values." And, "Explicating the parallel objectifications of women and animals makes the absent referents more visible."

Roughly translated, you are trying to say that even though there are no women present in the hunting stories you "researched," the hunters' prey are all symbolic of women.

I respectfully disagree. And I wish to offer a stunning confession. For the past few years that I have been deer hunting, I have been looking almost exclusively for male deer—remember, these are the ones we call "bucks." And the same thing goes for my pursuit of hogs. In fact, rarely do I stalk a female of any species I hunt. And the same thing goes for nearly all of my friends.

So, I think your present attempt to portray hunters as a bunch of sexists and rapists is wrongheaded. Clearly, given our penchant for disproportionately harvesting male animals, we are nothing but a bunch of closet homosexuals. And I think the feminists could do a lot for *Society & Animals: Journal of Human-Animal Studies* by penning a study called "The Queer Hunter: A Study of Homosexual Harvesting" for your next academic undertaking.

Then, perhaps you could pen a study on the disproportionate number of female babies aborted (read: harvested) worldwide every year. Since the feminists are the main ones pushing the abortion rate upward, perhaps the question that should be examined is: If most hunters are really gay, are most feminists really lesbians?

Update: *None of the authors offered a rebuttal to Dr. Adams's letter. Shortly after writing it, he killed a doe in the name of gender equality.*

Author's Note: *The original version of this paper ("Hunting as a Sexually Charged Activity: Evidence from Traditional Bow-hunter Magazine") was presented at the "Representing Animals Conference" at Brock University in Ontario, Canada, on November 13, 2003.*

46

HE'S CAMPAIGNING FOR BUSH!

D<small>EAR LYNNE:</small>

By now I'm sure you're aware that I'm writing a book lampooning feminism with a series of letters to whacky feminists. These letters are written and sent to feminists who have said dumb things in the hopes that they will reply by saying something even dumber. Armed with that knowledge, you may want to simply destroy this letter without responding. Furthermore, and unlike the other letters, this one contains no questions directed to the recipient.

When I complain that people are discriminated against on our campus because of their political views I usually expect to hear a denial. Recently, I made that very complaint (informally) on the Faculty Senate mailing list. After the complaint, you exercised your authority as Faculty Senate president by deleting me from the list. When another professor questioned you about the action, you responded by mentioning that I was "campaigning for Bush." Why did you interject Bush into the discussion? Do you suffer from Bush derangement syndrome? And does that negate or lend credence to my assertion that our campus discriminates against out-of-the-closet Republicans?

That's all. I just wanted to say "thanks." There's no need to respond because it will probably make you look even more intolerant than you do now. But, needless to say, I really hope to hear back from you.

Update: Dr. Adams is deeply disappointed that his lawsuit is keeping some of these letters from being mailed. This one will never be read by Snowden because she will not even read this book. In a 2004 interview with the Wilmington Star News *she characterized Dr. Adams as both mentally unstable and a pathological liar—all in response to his first book. This was shortly after she admitted (in the same interview) that she had not actually read the book.*

47

RED MAN FROM
THE MAILMAN

Dᴇᴀʀ ᴅᴏɴɴᴀ:

As I'm plugging away on my forthcoming book about feminism I thought about an incident that occurred in the department's main office last semester. You will recall that someone had placed a bag of Red Man chewing tobacco in your mailbox that had words to the effect of "Hey Sociologists: Suck on this!" written on the outside of the package. You probably also remember confronting me in the middle of the office to ask whether I was the one who left it in your mailbox.

It may come as some surprise when I tell you that I'm not writing to chastise you for behaving in an unprofessional manner. Given the fact that you chose to confront me—in an accusatory tone and in front of several students—I would certainly be justified in doing so. But, instead, I chose to write in an effort to better understand the feminist mind, particularly with regard to the subject of feminist stereotyping.

I know it probably offends you to hear me suggest that you were engaging in discriminatory behavior based on cultural stereotypes when you questioned your only male colleague from the Deep South after finding a bag of chewing tobacco in your mailbox. But, hopefully, the following questions will be sufficient to illustrate my point about your possible hypocrisy (assuming you teach students that stereotyping is wrong in your sociology classes):

> Suppose you found a slice of watermelon in your mailbox. Would you go find the first black person and ask him whether he put it there?
>
> Suppose you found a bagel in your mailbox. Would this cause you to question the first Jew you ran into in the office?
>
> Suppose you found a burrito in your mailbox. Would you go find a Mexican and question him about his possible involvement in planting it there?
>
> Suppose you found a fortune cookie in your mailbox. Would you confront an Asian and accuse him of planting it there.
>
> Suppose you found a slice of quiche or a pair of hair clippers in your mailbox. Would you go question the first gay man you saw?
>
> Suppose you found a condom in your mailbox with the words "planned parenthood" written on it. Would you go find the first feminist you saw and accuse her of placing it there?

Actually, Donna, last year someone did place a condom—with the words "planned parenthood" written on it—in my mailbox. Beside it there was a rude note asking me to use the condom so I wouldn't have children. It never occurred to me to confront you within earshot of students and ask whether you were the one responsible for putting it there. To do so would have been a form of cultural profiling. That's problematic, even if we ignore the whole issue of being unprofessional and uncollegial.

I hope I've made my point in this short missive. And I hope you don't really think I put that bag of Red Man in your mailbox. That would be odd, given that I am one-sixteenth Indian—although I would prefer you use the term "Native American."

Update: Dr. Adams only resembles a "Red man" when people try to embarrass him in front of his coworkers.

48

THE CABAL IS IN YOUR COURT

DEAR WENDY:

I am writing to give you a brief update on a controversy we were both involved in during the 2003–2004 academic year. You will recall that you were a member of a committee that was trying to force the College Republicans (CRs)—a group I advise—to sign an "antidiscrimination" clause stating that they would not prevent members of other political parties from seeking membership or holding office in their club. I took the view that the "antidiscrimination" clause was unconstitutional.

Put simply, I thought the United States Constitution's First Amendment guarantee of free association trumped the diversity policies in the UNCW handbook. You took the opposite view.

As you may or may not be aware, I helped organize a legal challenge to the same clause that was in effect on another UNC campus just 150 miles from here. I am referring, of course, to UNC-Chapel Hill.

I called or wrote letters to every religious group at UNC-CH that had been kicked off campus—and had their funds frozen—for refusing to allow members of different religious groups to join, vote, and hold office in their organization. For example, Christian groups were being required to admit Muslims, Buddhists, and atheists. They were even forced to let them run for office.

Thankfully, just a few weeks after I called two leaders of Alpha Iota Omega, a lawsuit was filed in federal court. And, as you may know, the very same antidiscrimination clause you supported was struck down via an injunction in federal court.

We were certainly proud of our legal victory although we were disappointed with the new "antidiscrimination" clause UNC-CH chose to put in place of the one we defeated in court. Unfortunately, our challenge to that clause was tossed out of court due to a technical issue. The merits of that clause will have to be tested later.

But I write not for the purpose of talking about future litigation. Instead, I write to talk about past trials in the court of public opinion—specifically, some of the things you said about our group during the controversy.

First of all, you editorialized sarcastically, in the student newspaper, that it was silly for the CRs to fear a hostile takeover by an angry "cabal" of hostile Democrats. Your tone suggested that someone had to be paranoid to think such a thing could actually happen. But it did, in fact, happen about two hundred yards from where you sat and wrote your remarks. That hostile takeover was back in 1988.

It is not my intention to chastise you for your historical ignorance of events that happened at UNCW in the 1980s. But something must be said about your historical ignorance of similar hostile takeovers that transpired in the 1950s. These were not mere pranks but, instead, expressions of rabid racism.

As you may or may not know, the KKK used to try to infiltrate the NAACP in the 1950s by joining the civil rights group in an effort to cast votes in favor of racial segregation. They sought to turn the antisegregation group into a pro-segregation group.

It was not until 1958 that the Supreme Court decided that the group could protect an implicit First Amendment freedom of association by discriminating on the basis of belief. This was despite the NAACP's status as a tax-exempt organization. In other words, they were allowed to engage in belief discrimination even while "using" public funds.

Our group never had a real concern that we would be victims of a similar hostile takeover. We just wanted to take the same principled stand against government interference articulated by the NAACP. Nonetheless, we respected your decision to side with the KKK in this matter.

In your column for the school newspaper you suggested that we were fighting for the right to discriminate in some broad manner. Your remarks were not well received by the group. In your defense, you did not go as far as Professor Veit of the English Department, who specifically accused us of trying to keep "blacks and Jews" out of the group. Nonetheless, your suggestion of some bigoted motivation did not go undetected.

This leads me to a rather simple request. Now that the courts have proven that you were wrong about the law and time has proven that you were wrong about the facts of the case—we have not tried to keep anyone out of the group due to factors unrelated to belief—would you consider a public apology?

We have already contacted Professor Veit to request an apology. He refused. We would like to give you a similar opportunity to atone for your misjudgment of the situation.

Update: Wendy hasn't written back just yet. But she did call Dr. Adams's office while he was away to ask whether the above was (a) actually written by Dr. Adams, or (b) a SPAM e-mail. Given the lack of any mention of Viagra or Asian kiddie porn, Dr. Adams assumes Wendy was just being difficult.

49

EVERYONE WHO'S NOT HERE, PLEASE RAISE YOUR HAND!

DEAR SUSAN:

I want to thank you for taking the time to place a copy of your new survey—one designed to measure "political bias" at UNCW—in my mailbox. I know it is your contention that there is no "political bias" at our university. Nonetheless, I hope you will consent to fill out a survey by someone who thinks there is.

It was with great interest that I noticed your survey—administered only to employees at UNCW—asked respondents whether they had experienced discrimination at various points in their career at our university. It was with even greater interest that I noticed one of those points was "hiring." This leads to a rather obvious question: How do you expect to find out how many people *were not* hired by the university—for political reasons or otherwise—by surveying only those who *were* hired by the university?

While you are contemplating my question, I hope you'll take the time to fill out this brief survey, designed especially for you:

1. Have you ever assessed the murder rate by conducting personal interviews asking people whether they have ever been murdered?

2. Have you ever taken the roll by simply asking your classes "how many of you are absent today"?

3. Have you ever run an ad in the school newspaper asking how many people are boycotting campus publications?

4. Have you ever administered a self-report survey asking why the recidivism rate is so much lower for suicide than for other forms of homicide?

5. Have you ever measured the frequency of PMS by conducting a survey of women who have had hysterectomies?

6. And, finally, have you administered IQ tests to any of the self-proclaimed "feminist scholars" at UNCW?

Thank you for your time.

Update: *Dr. Adams is still waiting for a response to the first letter he sent to Dr. Bullers. As soon as that happens, he will mail this one.*

50

WHY CAN'T YOU BE MORE LIKE WILLIAM F. BUCKLEY?

Dᴇᴀʀ ᴅɪᴀɴᴇ:

Have you ever had one of those days where you woke up and couldn't figure out whether the events of the previous day actually happened? I'm talking about a day so surreal that it caused you to question your sanity. For me, yesterday was one of those days. This is all a result of the conversation we had in your office, which, unfortunately, now appears to have been real.

I will probably never fully understand your decision to retain Donna, our feminist secretary who ridicules her husband's sexual performance and makes sexual remarks about male faculty members in the office. This is on days when she has not lost her temper, cried, and gone home early from work because someone disagreed with her.

Certainly, you have decided to retain her because she is a feminist. But you need to be careful because this woman is about to get you sued. In fact, she might get you sued by me.

It was simply outrageous of the previous chair to ask me to stop talking about my columns in the workplace because they might "offend" Donna. I knew that if I complied with the request she would find something else to "offend" her. And I was right.

When Donna started downloading, reading, and critiquing my column in the workplace—after she fought for a ban on their mere mention—she showed what feminists really seek in the marketplace of ideas: They want to criticize those who oppose feminism without any fear of having them respond. In other words, they seek to ban criticism of feminism altogether.

This is unacceptable. And that is why I criticized her in my national column, although I did not mention her by name. But, nonetheless, you had to call me into your office for a reprimand.

Diane, I was wholly unimpressed when, just seconds after I sat down, you reminded me that in three months as interim chair you had not yet "said anything" about my weekly columns. Nor was I impressed with the statement, "Mike, I know there's the First Amendment and all that."

The flippancy of your tone and hand gestures indicated that you fail to appreciate the price so many soldiers paid so we can have "the First Amendment and all that." Given the juvenile nature of your remarks, I'm surprised your sentences weren't littered with words such as "like" and "totally."

But, during our unfortunate conversation, you did ask a few serious questions that merit a response. In fact, you asked at least four questions, which I have highlighted below, and to which I respond with some questions of my own:

1. How can we respond to your columns, given that we don't have a platform of our own?

This is a typical example of the feminist worldview. You correctly note that there is a big power imbalance between me and the "we" to whom you refer—I assume this means all the feminists in our department who read my columns and disagree with them. But it has not always been this way.

Put simply, I have not always had a national column. I wrote a
regional column for a year—free of charge, mind you—until Rush
Limbaugh read one on the air and got me some free national exposure. This soon resulted in an offer to write a national column for
money.

If you want a national column, you're going to have to work—
perhaps without compensation like I did—to get one. Telling me "it
isn't fair" is not going to cut it. I'm not going to quit writing because
you don't like it. In fact, you are rewarding me by letting me know I
get under your skin. If you want a fair fight, get to work. Until then,
you're going to get worked over, especially if you keep calling me into
your office for these silly reprimands.

2. Why do you have to attack the poor secretary in your column, she
   has less power than the chancellor or another professor?

I was just trying to prove that she was reading my columns at work
and criticizing me. In other words, I wanted to prove that she really
didn't want to ban my column from work, just the positive discussion
of my columns, when she reported me to the previous chair. I think I
proved my point. And I did it without making fun of anyone's penis.
Are you beginning to understand what I'm trying to do with "the
First Amendment and all that"?

3. Why do you have to be so mean-spirited in your columns?

I have an idea, Diane. Rather than asking that I change my style of
writing because it is "mean" you could choose from two options: either
write one yourself that is not "mean," or stop reading my columns.

You stated in our meeting that "nearly everyone" in the department agrees that my column is "mean." That's a pretty strong argument against tenure. Don't you people have anything better to do than read columns you don't like?

4. Why can't you be more like William F. Buckley?

Diane, the idea that you want me to change styles of writing—specifically to be less "caustic" and more "cerebral" like William F. Buckley—only shows that I am succeeding with my attacks on feminist hypocrisy. If I were not, we would not be having this conversation.

Finally, Diane, I have written this detailed letter to preserve a record of your efforts to interfere with my constitutionally protected right to free speech—not to mention freedom of press, and free exercise of religion. If, during the course of the next year, I sense that you or anyone else is attempting to interfere with my First Amendment rights I will forward this letter to my attorneys and pursue litigation against you and the University of North Carolina at Wilmington.

But if you can resist reprimanding me for my views and asking me to curtail my First Amendment expression because—to quote you directly—"it would make things a whole lot more pleasant around the office," I will merely send this letter directly to you. No one else will have to see it and no litigation will be necessary.

I have a number of other questions I would like to ask. For example, "Wouldn't it be 'a whole lot more pleasant around the office' if you would just fire Donna" and "Why doesn't Donna just blast me on the NPR radio program she hosts rather than running to the chair crying." But, instead, I have a more serious question to pose as I conclude this letter.

Given that (a) early feminists were steadfastly opposed to censor-ship and abortion, and (b) modern feminists are steadfastly commit-ted to censorship and abortion, is it fair to say the feminist movement has lost its way? In other words, Diane, why can't you be more like Susan B. Anthony?

Update: Dr. Adams sued Dr. Levy in Spring of 2007.

51

MASTURBATION STUDIES

Dear DUKE UNIVERSITY WOMEN'S CENTER:

Recently, when I was passing by the office of a feminist professor (and department chair), I noticed a bumper sticker she had posted on the side of one of her filing cabinets. It said, "Vote Republican: It's Easier than Thinking."

I am so accustomed to hearing the "Republicans are Stupid" mantra (or, perhaps, wo-mantra) from feminists that I hardly think twice about it anymore. However, this morning when I read about your masturbation workshop I came up with an idea for a research project that might help explore the feminist assertion that they are really significantly more intelligent than the rest of the population.

My idea for a research project will involve attending the next Duke Women's Center seminar that provides guidance to women on techniques of masturbation. Specifically, I would like to administer IQ tests at the next seminar and, with your permission, also administer a brief questionnaire. I expect the results to show the following:

1. Feminists who need a seminar to learn to masturbate generally have IQs with two digits.

2. Women who need to learn to masturbate at a seminar generally vote Democratic.

3. Most of the women who attend these seminars are wealthy white students with SAT scores well below the Duke average. In other words, they were admitted to Duke as a result of "white female privilege."

4. None of the women in these seminars major in any of the so-called hard sciences. Most have a major that ends with the word "studies"—such as Gay and Lesbian Studies, African American Studies, or Women's Studies.

Thank you for your time. I look forward to working with you on this important project.

Update: The Duke Women's Center never responded to Dr. Adams. These women just don't have enough time on their hands.

PART IV

Why Feminists Hate Christians Who Go Shopping

52

THE SOUND OF SILENCE

Hello, kim.

I am in receipt of your September 21 memo, which begins by saying "I am disappointed that you declined my invitation to discuss personally the decision on your promotion (per e-mail: September 15, 2006). My preference is to communicate this information to you in person as I have done with similar personnel decisions in this Department since starting my term as Chair. Therefore, I am writing this memo to you as a professional courtesy."

That was an unexpected thing to hear, given that you stated the following (per e-mail: September 15, 2006): "Hi Mike, yes, of course I understand. I will do my best to prepare something in writing for you very soon. Given my schedule today, however, it is unlikely I'll be able to produce it today. Best wishes, Kim." This was in response to my request for a written explanation of the specific reasons for your decision to deny my promotion to full professor.

Your memo continues by saying "The decision to deny your application for promotion to professor was based exclusively on the promotion application and supplementary materials you submitted and my consultation with the senior faculty in accordance with existing

UNCW RTP policies and procedures. The senior faculty in the Department, in an overwhelming consensus, did not support your promotion to professor at this time."

The phrase that is of most importance in the paragraph I just quoted is "overwhelming consensus." I asked you the following (per e-mail: September 20, 2006): "Kim: A quick reminder that I am seeking a written justification for the decision to deny my application for full professor last week. Also, if I failed to mention it, I am seeking a count of the votes in favor and the votes against." So, in addition to not knowing the reasons for the denial, I am left without a sense of how close I came to being promoted.

Your memo continues by saying "Ultimately, though the Department Chairs are required to solicit feedback from and consult with senior faculty, the final decision rests with the Chair. As such, I take seriously my duty in this matter and find the lack of support from senior faculty compelling. In my view your record does not merit promotion to professor at this time."

Again, there seems to be a lack of understanding about the depth of what I am requesting. I wrote you (per e-mail: September 15, 2006) the following asking for just a small bit of guidance in this matter: "Kim: I am certain that a one-sentence summary, such as 'teaching evaluations and community service' would be feasible today. I expected a justification would be prepared before communicating the verdict." But you seem to be content saying that there was an "overwhelming consensus." But, of course, that does not tell me what the consensus was about. Was it about my teaching? Was it about my research? Was it about my service? All I really sought was one sentence from you.

Your memo concludes with the following paragraph: "Again, I remain available and willing to discuss this Departmental decision with you personally. I am also happy to provide guidance for you to develop a stronger record for a promotion application to professor at some point in the future. If you are interested in further dialogue with me, please schedule an appointment to see me."

I had planned to appeal the decision with a written response to your written justification. But now I have to base an appeal on my recollection of whatever you would say to me in an unrecorded conversation. Why, exactly, would you want me to base an appeal on a less accurate version of our conversation?

At risk of violating your requirement that any further dialogue take place in person, I nonetheless submit this humbly and respectfully for your consideration.

Update: Several days later, the chair wrote back to say that Dr. Adams was deficient in all areas—teaching, research, and service. After he read the letter, Dr. Adams stared at his 1998 UNCW Favorite Teacher Award for a few moments. Then he stared at the 2000 UNCW Faculty Member of the Year Award, which was also given to him for excellence in teaching. Next, he called his friends at the Alliance Defense Fund in Arizona.

53

REFUSING TO BE SILENCED

DEAR KIM:

As I was sitting here waiting for a reason (in writing) for my recent denial of promotion to full professor, I decided to take a look around the Internet to see whether you had made any public statements about due process that I could use to persuade you to give me a written statement for my appeal of your decision on my promotion. My thinking was that if my words could not persuade you, perhaps some of your own past statements could.

Given that you research wrongful convictions in the criminal justice system, I thought my chances of finding something persuasive would be good. So I did a Google search on the name "Kimberly J. Cook." I didn't find what I was seeking but I did find an interesting essay you wrote about an abusive relationship you were in back in the early 1980s. You claim that you were "battered, raped, starved to skeletal proportions, economically exploited, and emotionally controlled" by a man you lived with in New York. You even said that "when [you] wore [your] hair the 'wrong' way, he had to rape [you]."

I hope you will not mind my decision to quote extensively from your essay below. At the end of the quotations, I have a very serious question for you. I hope you will not ignore it as you have (so far) ignored my previous questions about the reasons for denying my promotion.

You state that your former lover "demanded sexual activities" you found "degrading and abusive." You say you were ashamed that "he violently raped" you and left you "bruised and forever traumatized." You say that he starved you and cursed you to lose weight and then beat you for wearing makeup that made you look like "a slut."

Because you expected him to kill you, family members helped you prepare to move back home. You report that you had few possessions—"clothes and some household items." And that your lover had cut all your clothing and left you "with only the clothes on [your] back." You report that he even destroyed your underwear.

In describing your "miraculous" escape from an abusive relationship, you paint a vivid picture of your last physical confrontation: He leapt over the coffee table and started punching me in the face, choking me, kicking me in the ribs, pounding my head on the floor. I managed to look out the window and a taxi had just dropped off a neighbor. I ran! I grabbed my luggage and begged the cabbie to take me to the bus station."

You attribute problems with drugs, alcohol, sex, and overeating to the pain of having been "raped, battered, starved, and utterly destitute." Your views on free will versus determinism are well summarized in these two sentences: "My self-destructive activities further punished my body with too much substance use and promiscuous sexual behavior. Society was telling me that the only value I had as a woman was through servicing men either with sex, food, or domestic service."

Kim, as much as I admire you for breaking out of your abusive relationship, I have a concern that your experiences may have left some emotional scars that presently impair your judgment. Is it at all possible that your experiences have also driven you to adopt an extremist political outlook that creeps into your decision making as a department chair?

Oh, and one more question: How did you look out the window and see a taxi cab dropping off a neighbor while your boyfriend supposedly was punching you, kicking you, choking you, and slamming your head into the floor? That was really quite a miraculous escape.

Update: This letter was never sent to Dr. Cook. Just before he was about to go to the mailbox, Dr. Adams's wife came in the room and started kicking, choking, and punching him. While he was getting his head slammed into the floor—all of this was because he forgot to go to the store to get toilet paper—he saw a taxi cab parked across the street. He ran outside, flagged it down, and convinced the driver to take him to Wal-Mart. Dr. Adams and his wife have since been reconciled.

54

TEARING DOWN THE WALLS
OF MALE DOMINANCE

H~I KIM~.

I just finished reading your essay called "Refusing to Be Silenced." I hope you don't mind that I have quoted from five paragraphs of the essay below. Also, if you don't mind, I have a question following each of the quotations that I hope you will take time to answer:

> I understood Marx experientially; I understood feminist theories experientially.

Do you think that the 100 million people murdered by communists between the years 1917 and 1989 "understood Marx experientially"?

> I seldom drink or use other substances, preferring the natural joys of great music, close friends, and my loving partner's arms around me.

You state that you seldom use "substances." I assume these "substances" are illegal drugs. Were you using illegal drugs at the time you decided to deny me promotion to full professor?

I am no longer silent on these and many other issues. I speak out, and I will continue to speak out because to do so is to tear down the walls of male dominance that control women's lives.

When you denied my application for full professor, did you feel like you were tearing down "the walls of male dominance that control women's lives"?

As feminist scholars, we must also work hard to break down those oppressive barriers to health and true happiness for women and children. As feminist scholars, we need to engage in radical self-care: speaking out, refusing to be silenced, validating our students who are feminist activists, sharing the "sourdough" empowerment inherent in feminist theory and feminist politics.

Do you believe that—in addition to "validating ... feminist activists"—you have an obligation to invalidate antifeminist activists like myself?

So, to the women who preceded me in feminist activism and scholarship, I owe a huge Thanks. Thank you for being strong in the face of great opposition. I am proud to be one beneficiary of your hard work. To the women who have shared my activism, either as cofounder of the International Coalition Against Sexual Harassment (formerly Sociologists Against Sexual Harassment), as coactivists with local shelters for battered women, as reproductive rights activists, or activist/scholars who publish in these areas, I say thanks for the sisterhood, the inspiration, and the laughter!

You stated that you wished to thank the feminist "activist/scholars" for "the inspiration, and the laughter." Kim, would you be offended if I took a moment to thank you for the inspiration to write this book and, also, to thank you for the laughter?

Update: The Berlin Wall is still down. And the feminists are still trying to explain why it was necessary in the first place.

For Further Reading:
> Kimberly J. Cook. "My Turn." *Sociologists for Women in Society* 18, 1 (Spring 2001).

55

TALKING DIRTY AND SHOOTING THE BIRDIE

D EAR KIM:

I am writing today to inform you of my decision to resign from the criminal justice faculty search committee. This decision is made entirely on the basis of my objections to the inclusion of another faculty member on that committee who has a track record of making improper, not to mention illegal, personnel decisions on the basis of factors such as political affiliation.

My objections to Diane Levy's presence on the committee can be traced back to her handling of a feminist secretary by the name of Donna. This was when Donna was on probation as a temporary worker seeking a permanent position as our second secretary. Diane was then the interim department chair.

From almost the beginning of her term of probation, Donna developed a habit of losing her temper to the point of yelling, crying, and, eventually, storming out of the office for hours at a time. Despite her rather obvious mental instability, Donna was, in fact, hired by Diane after the end of the probationary period.

I was troubled by Diane's decision because I sensed that she failed to control a staff member who clearly demonstrated her violent tendencies in the workplace simply because she was a fellow feminist. In fact, the only effort she made to control this woman was to ask others to change their behavior. Let me give you an example.

In April of 2004, Cecil Willis made the serious mistake of asking me not to mention the subject matter of my columns in front of Donna because it made her feel "uncomfortable." After this request was made, Donna continued for a period of six months to read my weekly columns in the office and to offer negative commentary—in the front of student workers, no less.

In response to this unacceptable situation—allowing Donna to critique the columns at work but not allowing me to discuss their "subject matter"—I wrote a column critical of Donna's emotional outbursts. The column also mentioned the fact that Donna was using the department e-mail list to promote the NPR radio segment she hosted—all of this after requesting a gag order banning me from discussing my column in the office.

But at no point in my column did I ever mention Donna by name. Nonetheless, she responded to it in a predictable manner; namely, by yelling, crying, slamming the door, and leaving the workplace for the last six hours of the day.

The point of my column was that speech codes, which protect people from feeling "uncomfortable" in the workplace, actually constitute a form of reverse Darwinism. I say this because they have a tendency to protect people who are emotionally unfit—like those who tend to leave the workplace crying—and punish people who are emotionally stable.

But Diane did not get the point of the column. In fact, she proceeded to reward the behavior of the least fit person in the dispute (Donna) by reprimanding me. This was all while Donna was on probation. And then Diane did something even more irresponsible. She hired Donna to fill the permanent secretarial position.

It should come as no surprise to you that Donna did not last very long. Diane was forced to fire Donna a few months later after she stormed across the office screaming "💣 you" at Sandy Rogers. Donna also had her middle finger extended. She was angry because Sandy went—on her lunch break, mind you—to see a pro-life display on the other side of campus. This, Donna said, was an example of how Sandy "pushed her religion on others."

Kim, even without all of these emotional outbursts, Diane should have had the good sense to fire this woman earlier when she started talking about her husband's erectile dysfunction in front of professors and students. But I fear that Diane was simply too much in agreement with Donna's feminism to make a rational decision about her fitness as a long-term employee.

And now I have learned that despite this poor handling of the secretarial hiring process, you recently placed her in charge of the hiring of another secretary in our department. I have also learned that she will be sitting on our criminal justice faculty search committee.

This is simply unacceptable. You may well question my assertion that Diane's handling of Donna's case was brought on by political favoritism bestowed on one feminist by another. But my circumstantial case against Diane is wildly bolstered by her inappropriate remarks in my year-end evaluation several months later. These remarks provide direct evidence of an inability to separate ideology from personnel matters.

To refresh your memory, Dr. Levy speculated in my 2005 evaluation that my political activities—such as speeches, columns, and media appearances—were interfering with my job performance. She suggested these activities were causing a decline in my research productivity.

Note that she did not say that my cigar smoking was interfering with my work performance. Also note that she did not say that my jogging was interfering with my work performance. You might also note that she didn't say my reading of literature was interfering with my work performance. And so on. And so on.

After failing to mention that my productivity lifts, not lowers, the average research productivity in the department, she also declined to attribute it to the things I do daily, like smoking cigars, jogging, and reading literature.

Instead, she said my political activities—a less frequently pursued endeavor—were the problem. These same activities—speeches, columns, and media appearances—yielded nothing but praise in annual evaluations written when I was a Democrat. (Please consult your files for immediate confirmation.)

This evaluation was really helpful for me as I looked back in an effort to interpret a remark Diane made to me in September of 2004. Her reference to an NRA dinner I attended as a "fascist pig dinner" seemed at first as if it might have been in jest. After all, the context of the remark was my communication to her that I would miss a party at her house to attend the NRA event.

But in the summer of 2005 a reinterpretation of the remark was in order after she wrote me up for my so-called political activities, as I just explained.

Let me conclude this missive with a qualifying statement; namely, that I understand you were not a witness to all of the aforementioned events. But you have seen some of what I'm talking about.

For example, you were present to hear Diane's remark that our community is comprised of nothing but people with "pot bellies and pickup trucks." Diane made that remark in response to a faculty member who suggested that our department should not sponsor a film about teenagers getting sex changes for fear of offending the community.

Diane's remark was significant but not for the reasons one might initially assume. The part of her comment making fun of the obese was silly given her own past struggles with obesity, but it was not significant. The part of her comment making fun of people who drive pickup trucks was also silly—and maybe a bit uppity for a sociologist—but it was not significant.

The significance of her comment was the suggestion that since the community is conservative, the department has an obligation to sponsor liberal speech as a means of creating balance. That's what she meant when she said we have to "challenge the standards of the community." But, certainly, if she were teaching at Cornell University in liberal Ithaca, New York, she would feel no corresponding obligation to "challenge the standards of the community" by providing balance in the form of conservative speech.

As you can see, Kim, I have given this matter considerable thought. And I hope you will respect my decision. I ask you to keep this entire communication between us—unless, of course, I should decide to waive the confidentiality I am requesting. After all, I would not want Diane to retaliate against me politically.

Or should I say that I would not want her to retaliate against me again?

Update: On advice of legal counsel, Dr. Adams did not send this letter to Dr. Cook. He remained on the search committee, which interviewed four candidates. All of the interviewees had breasts and wore makeup.

56

TITLE VII

To my esteemed attorneys at the Alliance Defense Fund:

I am certain that Dr. Cook will argue that all of these things are merely coincidental or imaginary. But, of course, I disagree. I believe that Dr. Cook is a bigot whose evaluation of my performance cannot satisfy the "straight face" test—or, for that matter, a jury. Soon we will find out if I'm right.

Gentlemen, perhaps I should have paid closer attention to a criminology professor at another university who warned me about Dr. Kimberly J. Cook's rejection of Christian doctrine.

Nonetheless, we did hire Dr. Cook. And that decision probably emboldened the others in our department whose dismissal of Christian beliefs I did not fully gauge when I interviewed for this job in 1993. Of course, at the time I was an avowed athiest wholly unconcerned with religious liberty in higher education.

After I took the job at UNC-Wilmington I was treated very fairly by my first chair, Dr. Steven J. McNamee. He was my boss from 1993 to 1996. In his annual evaluations of my performance, he called me a "master teacher" who had the "highest teaching evaluations in department history." He predicted I would win numerous teaching awards in the future. Steve is a liberal Democrat and a member of a liberal Catholic Church.

My second chair, Dr. Cecil Willis, was also very complimentary in his evaluations. He nominated me for my first teaching award in 1996. He also praised me publicly for the Dean of Student's Office teaching awards I won in 1998 and 2000. After I became an out-of-the-closet Republican and fundamentalist we had only one disagreement. That was in 2004, shortly before he stepped down as chair. Although a fairly liberal Democrat, Cecil joined the Baptist Church several years after his last promotion in our department.

But prior to the aforementioned disagreement with Cecil in 2004, I had numerous problems with the faculty. These problems began shortly after I "came out of the closet," so to speak, in the year 2000.

My first direct experience with, what I felt was, political retaliation came in the summer of 2000 when a feminist in our department, Dr. Lynn Snowden, removed me from the faculty senate mailing list. I have always assumed, but of course cannot prove, it was because I was "campaigning for Bush."

Counsel, I don't need to tell you that this was not an isolated incident. You are already familiar with the details of the 2001 action taken against me for some political statements I made in the wake of the attacks of September 11, 2001—statements made in response to a Marxist feminist student who blamed the attacks on U.S. foreign policy.

There were very few people following my case who believed that a college honors student, even though she was a Marxist feminist, would actually attempt to charge a professor with "libel" for simply characterizing a pro-socialist missive as "bigoted," "unintelligent," and "immature" speech. Even fewer people could believe that the UNCW administration would actually undertake a witch hunt against me, even going so far as to invoke their right to read my personal e-mails because they were on the university's system.

But that is what the administration did.

Fortunately for me, John Leo decided to make a national case of it with his column in *U.S. News & World Report*. Later, as the controversy exploded, the university explained that they had not turned over records of my correspondence to the Marxist feminist student and her mother, a Marxist feminist professor and UNCW administrator, but they admitted they read them.

Somewhere between UNCW's reading the e-mails and John Leo's column, Dr. Lynn Snowden decided to join in the fun.

It was on November 27, 2001, at the height of the controversy, when Snowden decided to go to the UNCW police and accuse me of entering her office. Specifically, the unhinged feminist claimed that I broke into her office to spray some sort of toxic substances.

I was not cleared of those charges until April of 2006. Though there was a costly police investigation, which included my interrogation and a physical investigation of the "crime scene" by the SBI, Snowden was never punished for her false accusations.

About six months after Snowden filed her baseless police report, I decided to start criticizing the problem of political correctness in higher education. Hardly able to believe that such incivility could go on in academia without some form of condemnation, I decided to heed Justice Brandeis's advice; namely, that "sunlight" could be among the most powerful of disinfectants.

When I published my first column, in the summer of 2002, criticizing my department and university for religious intolerance, the tension was immediately palpable. I remember one professor refusing to speak to me for several months after I published a column called "The Campus Crusade Against Christ." It wasn't just my imagination, either. Department Secretary Sandy Rogers, the only other openly Evangelical Christian in the department, said that the entire department was in an "uproar" over the column. In other words, they were unwilling to tolerate conservative speech, which said they were intolerant of conservative speech.

Despite the "uproar" caused by my columns, I decided to go up for promotion to the rank of full professor in 2004. I met with our then–interim chair, a sociologist named Diane Levy. Diane is an outspoken feminist, and a liberal Jew—ethnically, but not religiously, speaking.

During a brief meeting with Diane I told her of my interest in applying for promotion. I also told her that I would be putting a list of my research publications in her mailbox asking her to get back in touch with me to provide feedback as to whether my publications were sufficient for promotion. This is significant because it was just after I got my tenth refereed publication. Both previous chairs—McNamee and Willis—stated that ten (refereed publications) was a "safe" number for those seeking promotion to full professor.

Diane did not offer the feedback I requested. Instead, she remained silent for ten months until my year-end evaluation, in which she stated that she was concerned about a decline in my research productivity, which she attributed as an aside to my excessive political activity. I cannot help but wonder if the political activity itself was the real reason for her poor evaluation, and whether things would have turned out differently if I was campaigning for Kerry.

So, after the evaluation, I went to work and got an eleventh refereed publication before I tried to seek promotion again with our new chair, Kimberly Cook. Kim is a Marxist feminist and an atheist who has been openly critical of some Christian beliefs.

Despite her worldview, I am very surprised at the stunt Dr. Cook has pulled with regard to my promotion. After all, she was fair-minded enough to offer to delete a peer evaluation I got in June from a colleague who down-graded me on service for my "political activity." Not only that, but she helped clear my name of Snowden's false felony charge last April.

But something strange is indeed happening with this promotion. She has now taken the stance that it was deficient in every area: teaching, research, and service.

And this brings me to the reason for suing my Marxist feminist boss. She told me in August that the department was going to vote on my application in September. Then, after explaining my denial, she told me that there was no vote—and that none was required by the faculty handbook. When I later told Professor Randy LaGrange that I was judged deficient in all three areas, he emphatically asserted, "That isn't the way the department voted."

Randy's statement was not the first time I heard something that led me to believe Dr. Cook sometimes manipulated or disregarded faculty votes to suit her purposes. Dr. Rob Miller accused Dr. Cook of miscounting in a department vote on a new hire last spring semester. After a recount, Cook "acknowledged" she had miscounted by two votes—the errors were in the direction of the candidate Cook favored.

Dr. Reid Toth was a Republican woman in our department who was denied tenure the first semester Dr. Cook served as chair in our department. Toth has since taken a job at Western Carolina University. She has also accused Cook of misleading her new chair at WCU; specifically, telling him that Toth was denied tenure because she had only five refereed publications and needed six. Our department has never set a quota of six refereed publications for purposes of tenure.

Based on what I heard from Randy LaGrange and Dr. Rob Miller, I have also come to believe that Dr. Cook has sometimes manipulated or found an excuse to ignore a faculty vote that does not serve her purposes. Recently, she also seems to be establishing a paper trail that could be used in possible personnel actions against the two conservative Christians in the department.

Sandy Rogers, the only other Evangelical Christian Republican working in the department, recently received her first negative write-up—in the span of thirty years with the university—from Dr. Cook. The incident took place shortly after Sandy complained to Cook about the amount of overtime work she (Sandy) was doing. Kim said it was her choice to work overtime, urged her to just leave when the clock struck five, and, finally, said she was a "walking heart attack" in need of some rest and relaxation.

As a result, Sandy took an extra hour for lunch the next day—a mere fraction of the overtime she'd put in the previous week. For taking the extra hour off, Kim wrote her a reprimand and placed it in her personnel file.

When Sandy suggested she was being trapped into a mistake, and that she feared Cook was trying to create a paper trail to get rid of her, I thought she was overreacting. She also said she was contemplating retirement because of health problems such as weight gain and anxiety that she attributes to working with Cook. When we spoke, she specifically attributed this negative treatment to religious discrimination.

I began to take Sandy much more seriously later in the semester when Cook complained to the department about some people canceling class too often. At first, I did not think she was referring to me, specifically. After all, a feminist once canceled class for a whole week just to protest the Iraq War—and ran off antiwar posters on the office copier—with impunity. I had never canceled class for more than a day in my entire career.

Nonetheless, Cook stated (in a department meeting) that she was embarrassed when people would come into the office asking if Dr. So-and-so had canceled class that day and she (Cook) didn't know the answer. So I respected her request that we not cancel a class without telling her in advance. In fact, I scheduled my next two speeches—on the subject of how feminists use university policies to prevent free speech—on days when I did not have class.

Subsequently, my feminist boss wrote to say that my speeches—again, on the subject how feminists use university policies to prevent free speech—were in violation of university policies. This was because I missed a search committee meeting when giving one of the speeches.

Dr. Cook wrote me up and said I erred by not telling her in advance that I would miss the meeting, because it was one of my "regular campus duties." This sounds very reasonable, but for the following three reasons, it is not. In fact, it is discriminatory:

1. The policy she quoted comes from the "teaching" subfolder of the faculty handbook and, therefore, only applies to missing class.

2. The same week that she complained about my missing a search committee meeting because of "external professional activities" she granted a special request to an outspoken atheist in our department. He asked to do his last two years of work at UNC-Wilmington (on phased retirement) by only teaching online classes. During this time he would live and hold down a full-time job in Columbus, Ohio. He was excused from all meetings and committee assignments for two solid years.

3. Less than one month later we would find ourselves desperately scrambling to hire two faculty members as potential candidates were being hired left and right by other schools. Nonetheless, Kim

would postpone a search committee meeting for several days while she was on Christmas vacation in Maine. Kim was supposed to be back for her "regular campus duties" on January 5.

Update: *The attorneys at the Alliance Defense Fund did respond to this letter. That's largely due to the fact that they are not feminists.*

57

SEEKING NUDE SEPTUAGENARIANS (NO BREAST IMPLANTS, PLEASE!)

Dᴇᴀʀ ᴘʀᴏꜰᴇꜱꜱᴏʀ ʙᴏᴏᴛʜ:

I am writing to express my deep disappointment with your contribution to a growing problem in America. The problem can best be described as a diminishing view of our churches as holy places from which we can escape the sins of the flesh-centered world. Because of people like you, many of our houses of God are looking more like houses of ill repute.

For example, the other day in church I noticed a young woman entering the sanctuary—about five minutes into the service—wearing the kind of clothing one would expect to see at a dance bar. Her breasts were hanging out of her shirt and her thong underwear was climbing high above the back of her pants. If it got any higher, it would have covered the spread-eagle tattoo on her lower back.

The friend who joined her—about ten minutes later in the service—was wearing one of those low skirts that a girl can only wear if she's recently shaved her pubic hair. I was going to say something to the girl but her cell phone went off during the Lord's Prayer and she had to leave early.

But, as inappropriately as these girls were dressed, at least they were actually wearing some form of clothing. That's why I'm less disappointed in them than I am in you. By organizing a nude church calendar—complete with twelve naked female members of your congregation—you have taken disrespect for God to an entirely new level.

Even worse than actually producing such a calendar is your decision to use nude women covering their breast and genitalia between the ages of forty-two and seventy-four. By using these older women, some will think you are just trying to be cute. But since you are a feminist professor, I know you are really trying to send a serious message; namely, that the notion that "young is beautiful" is a by-product of a patriarchal, male-dominated society.

Your nude-calendar stunt shows that you are always careful not to offend the timeless principles of feminism even when you are openly insulting the Creator of our universe. In that sense, isn't it fair to say that feminism is your real religion?

I am wondering whether you can verify the rumor that you plan to sell these calendars inside your church to raise money for new church kitchen renovations. I am also wondering whether you are at all concerned that you are going to hell.

Update: There has been no response from Professor Booth. She can't seem to handle the naked truth.

58

THE FEMINIST WHO STOLE CHRISTMAS

Dᴇᴀʀ ʀᴏsᴇᴍᴀʀʏ:

I write to you with a heavy heart this Christmas because, quite frankly, you have ruined my entire holiday season. And it was all because you, like most feminists, simply cannot take a joke. Let me refresh your memory if you don't already know what I'm talking about.

Last Christmas, you sent out a holiday greeting that made no mention of the word "Christmas"—presumably because you did not want to offend anyone by using a word that is an extension of the word "Christ." The card actually offended more people than you imagined because it mentioned the word "diversity" and called attention to some of your accomplishments as chancellor.

I was not the only one who thought the card made you look like a pompous 🐴. Nor was I alone in my objection to your effort to use the card to portray our campus as "safe." It would have made more sense to mention Jesus than all of these other issues having nothing to do with Christmas. Besides, everyone still remembered the teenage student who was raped, sodomized, and murdered in a dorm on campus the year before. Hence, the Christmas card that mentioned campus safety but not Christ made you look both pompous and pretty silly, too.

But I do wish to apologize for two things I said in a radio interview last year that probably offended you. First, I noted that using the phrase "Happy Holiday" instead of "Merry Christmas" was a silly way to avoid a "separation of church and state" issue because "Holiday" stands for "Holy Day."

Second, I also made fun of you publicly for attending the *Vagina Monologues* and then, just nine months later, refusing to utter the word "Christ." During a local radio interview I stated that the feminist view that the word "Christ" is more offensive than the word "vagina" is evidence that few feminists have three-digit IQs.

So, for both of those things, I'm really sorry, Rosemary.

But, nonetheless, I think you overreacted when you took my name off your Christmas ... I mean, holiday greeting card list this year. Every single faculty and staff member at the university received a personalized electronic greeting card except me.

When Rob Miller showed me his "Happy Holidays, Rob" greeting card, I was burning with envy. And that's why my entire holiday (as opposed to holy day) has been ruined.

In all seriousness, though, I did not think you could make a bigger of yourself than you did with last year's Christophobic greeting card. But now your adolescent move to actually take the time to delete me from your card list—for merely expressing my First Amendment rights—is being read in a nationally published book. What could you possibly do to top this next year?

Think about it for a while and give me your answer by Vagina Day. And, by the way, do you remember when the feminists still let us call it Valentine's Day?

Update: The UNCW administration renamed the "Christmas Tree" the "Tree" in 2005 to avoid offending people. After Dr. Adams criticized them publicly for the change they stopped referring to "the tree" altogether.

That is why, in 2005, the website showed them decorating the tree in a picture with a caption below mentioning "the Tree." In 2006, the website showed them decorating the tree in a picture with a caption saying they were decorating "the House." Referring merely to the house in which the tree was sitting, but not the tree itself, was supposed to (a) keep people from getting offended while (b) keeping Dr. Adams from making fun of the chancellor.

Needless to say, the effort failed on both counts. And, needless to say, this letter was never sent to Rosemary. That's because Rosemary forwarded the first two letters Dr. Adams sent to her to men and asked them to respond for her. In response, Dr. Adams did send her a bumper sticker saying "Never send a feminist to do a man's job."

59

I WANT TO BE A UNICORN

Professor Conway:

I am writing regarding the letter you sent to my chancellor, dean, and department chair characterizing me as "transphobic" for my public opposition to the transgendered lifestyle. I am inclined to view my opposition to alternate lifestyles as an expression of my religious views, which are protected by the First Amendment. This leads me to ask the following questions:

You consider it normal if a man decides he is a woman and has his penis surgically removed. You even consider his critics to be "transphobic." What if he decides he is a unicorn and has the penis reattached to his forehead? Is he still normal? Do his critics suffer from some sort of phobia?

Update: Dr. Adams never received a satisfactory answer to his deep and penetrating question. He'll probably never feel fulfilled until he has.

60

MY CONVERSION TO MARXIST FEMINISM

Good morning, Kim.

I have some good news and some bad news for you today. First the good news! After eighteen months of being at odds with you over your support of Marxism and feminism I have decided that I, too, am going to become a Marxist feminist. This is not a joke like the time I said I was getting a sex change to qualify for a position in the Office of Campus Diversity. I'm dead serious about this!

My decision to become a Marxist feminist happened during the middle of our last department meeting. You will recall that we were trying to decide whether to start searching for someone to fill a new faculty position given to us by the dean, this year (as we are already searching to fill two other faculty positions), or whether we would start a new search at the beginning of next year.

In the midst of trying to make this rather simple decision, I noticed that my colleagues were getting confused and frustrated constantly. Several times, Donna King, a fellow Marxist feminist, had to stop and ask what we were talking about and what we had decided thus far. And then, just when it seemed we had made a decision,

---

someone would throw out a new suggestion and we would soon be going in circles again.

In the midst of all this confusion, it occurred to me that this small group of socialists—who cannot make a simple decision about a simple issue—is the same group of people who have enough faith in themselves to believe that they can create a Utopian society. Their perfect world will also, of course, be based on the teachings of their Lord and Savior, Karl Marx.

So it occurred to me that you guys could use a little help. Hence, I am converting to Marxist feminism. And this brings me to the bad news.

Rather than being one of those Marxist feminists who merely wears a Che Guevara T-shirt and combat boots, I intend to make Marxism a part of my everyday life. And I plan to start with my class grading policies.

Instead of assigning grades according to merit, I plan to simply add all of my student's scores together and divide by the total number of students. Since I grade on a bell curve, this means that every student—every semester in every class—will receive a grade of "C." Nothing would please Karl Marx more than knowing that regardless of talent or effort everyone will get the same outcome in my classes.

Of course, this means that a large portion of my students—the ones who knew they were better than average—will come pounding on your door at the end of the semester. But, looking on the bright side, all the slackers and idiots will leave you alone knowing full well that they got a good deal under my new communist regime.

While this may cause some inconvenience to you initially, you may take some solace in the fact that eventually, after the word gets out about my grading policies, only the worst students will sign up for my classes. And all of these kids will be thrilled to get a grade of C.

(If you don't believe that socialism attracts the lazy and dim-witted, again, just reflect back on our last department meeting.)

After I implement my new policies in class, I will do the same with regard to peer evaluations. For years, I've been giving my colleagues high (and variable) marks on their teaching, research, and service ratings. But, from now on, I plan to give everyone a five (the scale ranges from one to nine) regardless of what kind of a year they had.

When they come complaining to you just remind them that, compared with professors in other disciplines, sociologists and criminologists are actually less intelligent than average. Therefore, their "average" rating is really quite generous.

And, finally, I have some really bad news pertaining to my last commitment to the spread of Marxist feminism. It has to do with faculty salaries.

As I was looking at the list of faculty salaries for the year 2006–2007, I noticed that you are making around $40,000 more than I am making per year. And, since you are a Marxist, this clearly runs contrary to your beliefs about the distribution of wealth in a Utopian society. But, fortunately, there is a solution.

Rather than waiting for the rest of the world to convert to communism—that whole Berlin Wall incident in 1989 sure was a setback—you can start to form a communist society right here and right now in America with one simple action. All you have to do right now is to set an example by writing me a personal check for $20,000.

And just as soon as pay equity is established between us, I'll go find someone less fortunate and write a check to him. If you don't believe me then you really aren't a true Marxist feminist. Any Utopian society assumes that people are sufficiently full of good will to make things work.

All it will take to achieve our goals is that we stop to imagine the whole world living in peace. It's just as simple as John Lennon makes it out to be if you just have faith in your fellow man (and woman!) and, of course, in Karl Marx. So go ahead and write me that check for $20,000. Show the whole world you aren't some hypocritical feminist in combat boots. If you'll just take the plunge, the next four-dollar latte is on me!

Update: During a recent job search, Dr. Cook paid for Dr. Adams's dinner. As a result, he plans to redraft and send this letter with a request for only $19,960. Dr. Adams truly enjoyed his steak and shrimp dinner and hopes one day to live a lifestyle every bit as lavish as the twenty-first-century followers of Karl Marx.

PART V

Conclusion

61

A LETTER TO ABIGAIL ADAMS

January 10, 2007

It seems strange, perhaps, to conclude this book with a letter addressed to Abigail Adams. After all, you cannot read what I have to say, although I wish you could. The reader has come to understand, however, over the course of these pages, that there is little similarity between the earliest feminists who helped shape this country into the greatest the world has ever known and those who call themselves feminists today.

Perhaps one of the greatest true feminists I have ever known is a woman by the name of Virginia Rester. She was born in 1918 and is, therefore, someone you've never heard of before. She achieved a lot for a woman living in the middle part of the twentieth century—a century you did not have the great fortune of witnessing in your lifetime.

Virginia was born in a small town in Mississippi and, surprisingly, was able to get not just a high school diploma but a junior college degree. This was near the end of the Great Depression when few women in Mississippi finished high school. Virginia amazed everyone when she landed a good job with the federal government working at an air force base on the Mississippi Gulf Coast. She worked for thirty-three years before retiring in 1973 with a full federal pension.

While it was not then customary for women to hold positions of authority, she did so successfully. She ran the personnel office at that air force base with the full respect of men and women alike. She did so by setting high expectations for herself and others, by never losing her temper, and by always rewarding good behavior with a compliment and a smile.

It was about ten years before her retirement that Virginia entered into the lives of my family and forever changed our world for the better. She became a loving wife, mother, and grandmother to people whose lives had been touched by a terrible tragedy.

It was in the year 1962—just two years before my birth—when my maternal grandmother Nell Myers Rester died at the age of forty-eight from cancer. Her husband, Monroe Rester, was devastated as was his daughter, Marilyn, and sons, Jimmy and Johnny. But the same gracious God who gave him Nell, also gave him Virginia just a year later.

Suddenly, this woman who had been a "career woman" for twenty-three years was thrust into the role of wife and mother for the very first time. And within a year or so she would play the role of grandmother to me. It never really occurred to me that she was not my biological grandmother or that she somehow was not "real."

I first came to realize what a wonderful woman she was in the summer of 1980. The occasion was my brother's wedding. It was just one night before the wedding that I overheard Monroe tell my paternal grandmother, Blanche, that he was undeserving of a loving wife like Virginia. He described her as a wife who put up with all of his flaws and loved everyone unconditionally, always giving and always placing the needs of others before her own.

In 1984, Virginia's willingness to give of herself would be tested.

Monroe lost his left leg and nearly his life and was confined to a bed until he passed in late 1988. During those long four and a half years she waited on him constantly. When he passed, people talked about how Virginia had secured a place in heaven near to the throne with her unrelenting care for her husband.

After Monroe's funeral, and just before I departed from her house to head back to graduate school, Virginia pulled me aside to ask me a very serious question. She wanted to know whether I would still come to see her now that my real grandparent was gone. I laughed as I assured her that I would be back for the next holiday and, perhaps more important, her next batch of shrimp gumbo.

Virginia Rester was laid to rest today, just a few hours before I sat down to write this letter to you. Although she has passed, her influence is still felt. In fact, I assume it was really my relationship with Virginia that caused me to say "yes" when my fiancée asked whether I would consider adoption in the event of a problem with fertility. I learned from Virginia that a "real" parent doesn't have to be a biological parent.

It was around the end of our second year of marriage that we realized the surgery would not work and that we would never have another pregnancy—our only one ending in a miscarriage. And so we did what married couples with no children do. We watched a lot of television.

One night, there was a documentary on cable television that featured young Asian girls working as prostitutes in Thailand. Some were as young as five or six. Of course, we had already known of the problems concerning young girls, infanticide, and sexual slavery in China. But it began to occur to us that the problem was more widespread than we had previously believed. So we began to seriously consider adopting a little girl from Asia.

The following summer, we visited an orientation meeting for an adoption agency in Raleigh, North Carolina. We loved it. And we all but decided to adopt. But, of course, there was the issue of money.

We were given a very specific amount needed to secure the adoption of a child from Vietnam, the country we chose for a number of different reasons. And just as we began to talk about where the money would come from a funny thing happened. My agent, D. J. Snell of Orlando, Florida, called out of nowhere to tell me that Penguin USA was offering a book advance for the exact amount of money the agency had quoted! The book would be called *Feminists Say the Darndest Things*.

So, how ironic is that? I would help save a child from abortion and communism by writing a book criticizing feminists for their love of abortion and communism. It was truly an act of divine intervention to have these funds just fall out of the sky. After all, UNC-Wilmington, which pays its employees to abort children but not to adopt them, would not be there to help me.

And so I started to write my letters to feminists knowing full well that few, if any, would bother to write back. It was my intent to write letters so devastating to feminist hypocrisy that they really could not be answered. Thus, I would demonstrate with these letters not only the extremism of modern feminist positions, but the unwillingness of feminists to discuss them.

But even I may have underestimated the censorious nature of twenty-first century feminism. The day before I was to be voted on for full professor, I finalized my contract with Penguin and placed a copy of the contract (minus the financial information) in my full professor application packet. The next day I was denied promotion.

Shortly after my denial, I started to give a series of lectures called "How to Win Friends and Irritate Feminists." The lectures discussed how feminists use university policies to try to trump free speech, but only when the speech is critical of feminism. When my Marxist feminist chair heard about the speeches she tried to use university policies to stop them. These women are nothing if not predictable.

But, fortunately, in the process of denying the promotion and trying to stop the speaking tour, the feminists have made a few missteps—or, perhaps, Ms-steps. Hence, there will be a federal lawsuit filed in just a few days.

Filing a federal lawsuit, particularly one that may start with a Washington, D.C., press conference, sounds at first like it will be the highlight of the year. But, actually, it will probably be the third most exciting thing I will do. The second will be the release of the book on feminism. That should be sometime in February.

But, without question, the most exciting thing that will happen this year will be your new mother's trip to Vietnam. She will be heading over there (hopefully) soon and will stay there for two weeks before bringing our little girl home.

And when the plane touches ground I will be waiting there in the airport with open arms, holding back tears of joy, and trying to tell you in my best broken Vietnamese, "I love you, Abigail. I am your father. Welcome home, my beautiful angel. Welcome home."

ABOUT THE AUTHOR

WHEN HE RECEIVED HIS PH.D. IN 1993, MIKE S. ADAMS WAS both an atheist and a Democrat. Later that year he was hired by the University of North Carolina-Wilmington as a professor in the criminology program. A few years later, Adams abandoned his atheism and also became a Republican. He also nearly abandoned teaching when he took a one-year leave of absence to study law at UNC-Chapel Hill in 1998. In April 2000, after returning to teach at UNC-Wilmington, Adams won the Faculty Member of the Year Award (issued by the Office of the Dean of Students) for the second time.

After his involvement in a well-publicized free speech controversy in the wake of the 9/11 terror attacks, Adams became a vocal critic of the diversity movement in academia. After making appearances on shows like *Hannity & Colmes*, *The O'Reilly Factor*, and *Scarborough Country*, Adams was asked in 2003 to write a column for Townhall .com. He soon became a national leader in the campus free speech movement.

Dr. Adams specializes in turning local abuses of the First Amendment into national news stories. His columns are e-mailed overnight to 200,000 readers on Town Hall's Opinion Alert. The next day they receive up to 100,000 hits on Town Hall before they are reprinted on websites like Front Page and Human Events. His columns have also appeared in print publications such as the *Washington Times*.

Radio talk shows have also started reading Mike Adams's columns on the air. Examples include Rush Limbaugh, Sean Hannity, and Neal Boortz (a show on which Dr. Adams regularly appears). On one occasion, a reading by Sean Hannity resulted in 20,000 e-mails to a Student Government Association engaging in religious viewpoint discrimination.

Dr. Adams also works for the Young America's Foundation as a campus political speaker. His appearances have ranged geographically all the way from Oregon to New Hampshire. Some of Adams's speeches, such as an address to the Yale Law School College Republicans, have been aired on C-SPAN.

Today Adams enjoys the privilege of expressing himself both as a teacher and as a writer. In his spare time, he loves making fun of feminists with his antifeminist wife, Krysten. Dr. Adams is also an avid hunter and reader of classic literature. In 2004, he published his first book, *Welcome to the Ivory Tower of Babel*.